Education, Recession
and The World Village

EDUCATIONAL ANALYSIS
General Editors: Philip Taylor and Colin Richards

CONTEMPORARY ANALYSIS IN EDUCATION SERIES
General Editor: Philip Taylor

ST. MARY'S COLLEGE   TRENCH HOUSE

This book is issued in accordance with current College
Library Regulations.

DATE DUE AT LIBRARY LAST STAMPED BELOW

Contemporary Analysis in Education Series

Education, Recession and The World Village: A Comparative Political Economy of Education

Edited and Introduced by
Frederick M. Wirt
University of Illinois
Champagne-Urbana,
USA

Grant Harman
University of New England
Armidale, Australia

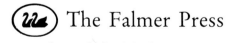 The Falmer Press

(A member of the Taylor & Francis Group)
London and Philadelphia

UK   The Falmer Press, Falmer House, Barcombe, Lewes, East Sussex. BN8 5DL.

USA   The Falmer Press, Taylor & Francis Inc., 242 Cherry Street, Philadelphia. PA 19106-1906.

First published in 1986

Library of Congress Cataloging-in-Publication Data

Main entry under title:

Education, recession, and the world village.

(Contemporary analysis in education series ; 11)
Includes index.
  1. Education — Economic aspects — Addresses, essays, lectures.
2. Education and state — Addresses, essays, lectures. I. Wirt, Frederick M. II. Harman, Grant Stewart. III. Series.
LC65.E33 1986 379 85-31099
ISBN 1-85000-081-6
ISBN 1-85000-082-4 (pbk.)

Jacket designed by Leonard Williams

Typeset in 11/13 Garamond by
Imago Publishing Ltd, Thame, Oxon

Printed in Great Britain by Taylor & Francis (Printers) Ltd, Basingstoke.

Contents

Content

General Editor's Preface

The assurance of the modern state is its economy. Shake it and the result sets in train unforeseen consequences to the fabric of the state: to its political, social and educational arrangements. This book seeks to explore the effects of such a 'shake', or recession, on the educational arrangements of eight modern states, some small, some large, some old, some new. It does so drawing on the understanding of people who have a close knowledge of the nations concerned from Hong Kong and Australia, from the United States and Nigeria and from the United Kingdom to China.

To bring to bear a common perspective across an international canvas on how the world recession has impinged on educational policy-making is no easy task, but it has been more than achieved by the authors of this book. Moreover, the authors have made one thing more than evident: the economy of the world in which we live today is all of a piece. The world is indeed a 'global village'. What affects the economic fabric of one country affects that of all others and as educational systems are integral to the workings of modern societies, they too are stressed. It is the singular value of this book that just how nations adjust their educational systems to meet the stress is brought into focus in a distinctive and scholarly fashion.

Philip H. Taylor
University of Birmingham
England
July 1985

Introduction: Comparing Educational Policies and International Currents

Frederick M. Wirt
University of Illinois, USA

Grant Harman
University of New England
Armidale, Australia

This volume is an effort to understand the effects of an international recession upon educational policy systems of different kinds of nation states. This introduction posits the concept of international independence, sets out the recession phenomenon, and explains the framework of the separate analyses that follow.

World Events and National Effects

The interdependence of the international community has become a commonplace of social analysis, and even at the popular level there is growing awareness of Marshall McLuhan's 'world village'. This relationship is not merely one of communication of events, fads, styles and artifacts among people of diverse cultures. The world village means more than the availability of designer jeans, rock albums and cinema to huge audiences across national borders.

Rather, actions important for the life and well-being of national systems can spread around the world. Such actions have consequences for social structure and public policy of nation states; these events and actions mock national limits. Such are seen in the international effects of a national event like an invention, for example, the atom bomb during World War II or the diode and chip in post-war computer technology. National, political and economic systems may filter these influences through their particular ideologies. But whether capitalist or socialist, less or more developed in their economy, democratic or authoritarian — all systems must react to such a singular, boundary-spanning change in the international environment.

Another class of such changes arises not from the action of a single nation, but from a simultaneous set of events arising among nations at the same time. War is the best example of this multiple-based, international relationship. It is commonplace now that societies change after wars, no matter the winner or loser — and in a future nuclear war, of course, the change would be total because no one would win.

A far less traumatic multiple action is a world recession. Readers are aware of the consequences of this phenomenon during the 1930s. That 'Great Depression' not only spawned fascism and the subsequent World War II, but it also wrought severe damage to individual lives and social structures within many nations. In this book we explore such a multiple-based phenomenon in order to trace its influence upon educational policy systems of different nations.

The World-Wide Recession

The last quarter of the twentieth century opened with a recession among all the modern nations that lacked independent, fossil-fuel sources. The birth of OPEC in 1973 and its raising of oil prices had devastating impacts upon the energy portions of budgets of all public and private agencies in both the less and more developed nations. That event is usually attributed to having caused subsequent inflation, unemployment, and cut in the growth rate of gross national products (GNP) which followed. As this is not an economic analysis, we do not carry the 'cause' of this recession any further, but the effects upon national economies were widespread. Figure 1 provides a graphic, brief sketch of those effects upon major capitalist nations, employing the single, most telling indicator of national economies, the GNP. The growth rate of GNPs in all these nations dropped immediately, some fell farther than others, all rebounded somewhat, but all fell again in a second wave of the recession, roughly from 1978 to 1983. All but the United States economy still feel its effects in 1985.

Figure 1

Changes in real GNP

In percentage change from previous year

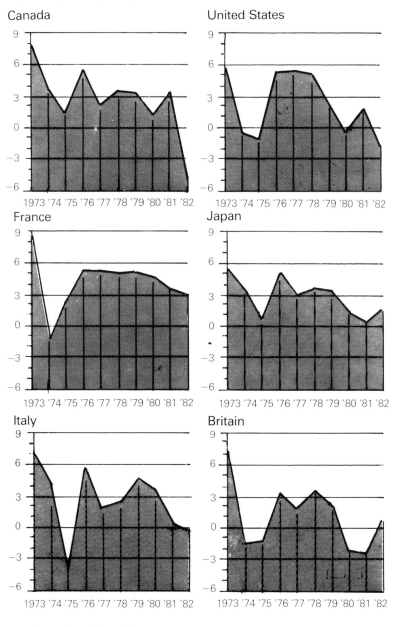

Canada

United States

France

Japan

Italy

Britain

Source: Chicago Tribune, 12 September 1983

Within each nation shown in Figure 1, and elsewhere, party governments struggled to deal with the recession. Often, party control rotated, but the newcomers to power were no more successful than those out of power. Ideological debates over the political economy raged within the mixed economies of modern democracies. In the United Kingdom and the United States, governments dedicated to the fiscal policies of John Maynard Keynes alternated with those dedicated to the monetary policies of Milton Friedman. Unfettered capitalism thrived in Hong Kong, while government-subsidized capitalism flourished in Japan. Less developed nations, dependent upon external resources for economic development, had to pay inflated prices for them. Socialist economies, less open to the world market and more inward-oriented to their bloc economy, may have resisted the drag of this international recession.

In this picture we can see diverse nations altering economic policies to deal with this international, boundary-spanning phenomenon. Could it also have had effect upon the educational policies of these nation states?

The Prism of National Qualities

The flow of extramural influences into national systems are necessarily affected by their national qualities. The latter operate like a prism, refracting and adapting those influences, without blocking all of them. At least three of these national qualities can have screening effects — economic resources, educational public policy-making processes, and dominant national values.

Economic Resources

The straightforward proposition is that an international recession must affect the revenues and expenditures of national budgets. If so, did this effect subsequently alter the flow of funds to its educational system? Or alternatively, some aspects of a national economic system can buffer the impact of an international recession, resulting in only limited consequences for educational spending. To examine such differential effects, nations were included in this study which were both capitalist and socialist, developed and less developed, rich and poor, and so on.

Educational Policy-Making

Faced with a recession, national leaders could alter the decisional processes of school government. There could be changes in those processes among national agencies of government, between central and peripheral governments, between or among political parties, and among the roles of educational professions and political leaders. Or again, buffered against external constraints like a recession, a nation's decisional processes could be unaffected. Such differences were sought among nations that were both federal and unitary, whose national governments were both presidential and parliamentary, and which had one-, two-, or multiple-party systems.

National Values

Implicit in the foregoing is the possibility that such an international event could change a nation's values about education itself. For example, in a constricting national economy, the resulting competition for limited resources might push funding of education lower on the priority list; alternatively, its place might be maintained in the funding picture. Both possibilities demonstrate the value basis of such budget decisions. In particular, could this recession and its national pressures alter views of education in investment vs. consumption terms? Or shift its focus from mass, comprehensive education to a system fostering elite, technological training for smaller numbers?

Effects on Selected Policy Outcomes

Authors in this study were also asked to focus upon a small set of educational policy issues that might run across some or all nations in order to determine how the recession affected them. Of course, not all issues were expected to appear, to be contentious, or to show effects in all nations studied.

1   Have educational leaders had to defend the role of education in society differently in the face of contracting resources, compared to a prior period of expanding resources? If so, what were the grounds of the attack and the defense?
2   Related to the first query, did there emerge fault-finding criticisms of education over the preparation of students for

later work life? If so, what were the charges and the responses?

3 Did there develop a competition for educational resources between government and the private sector? Did such criticisms as noted in the first two issues above generate rethinking of which sector could more effectively educate a nation's young? Or, alternatively, despite criticisms of the methods and results in schooling, did the basic educational structure remain immune from attack?

4 Among the challenges to education in this period, did attention focus upon the retention rates of students in secondary and higher education? If school budgets become constricted nationally by forces traceable to the international world, what questions are raised about the amount and length of education for the nation's young?

5 What special issues arose that were indigenous to each national culture, and did these reveal commonalites across nations? If so, these, like the preceding policy queries, might demonstrate both similar responses to international events as well as cultural variations in those responses.

Plan of the Enquiry

Philip H. Taylor, Editor of this series and Professor of Education at the University of Birmingham, accepted the co-editors' suggestion to solicit scholars familiar with the finances and government of education in selected nations to answer these queries. We first selected nations that fit certain criteria of nationhood, criteria which might have theoretical relevance for understanding national responses to international events. These criteria were:

1 National government, presidential vs. parliamentary.
2 Economic system, capitalist vs. socialist, developed vs. less developed, rich vs. poor.
3 Center-periphery relationships, federal (center vs. periphery strong) and unitary (center vs. periphery strong).

Against these criteria we evaluated a set of nations, from which the following were selected: Australia, Canada, Hong Kong, Nigeria, Papua New Guinea, People's Republic of China, United Kingdom and United States. The Union of Soviet Socialist Republics was first included but had to be dropped due to delays in preparation.

The co-editors then solicited scholars to write along lines suggested by the preceding sections and within a limited space (of course, all would wish more space). Additional charges given the authors included not originating their own research for this effort but rather summarizing the best research on their nations. The audience, we suggested, would be wider than their own national specialists in education but rather those similarly located in education and government around the world. A useful bibliography of sources was requested. The authors' names and affiliations appear at the head of each analysis.

The contributions were reviewed by the co-editors, revisions were suggested in a few cases, and time permitted updating events and analyses; delays arose which are natural to such international collaborative efforts. We contributed this introduction and the summary, comparative chapter. In the following, the organization of nations is alphabetical, because more than one scheme of organizing them exists, all useful.

We hope the results contribute to the literature on the world village, and to the continuing wisdom of John Donne, 'No man is an Iland, intire of it selfe; every man is a peece of the Continent.' (sic).

1 Australia

F.J. Hunt,

Monash University, Australia

A primary consequence of the period of economic constraint since the mid-1970s has been the wide acceptance of the significance of the economy to other areas of social activity such as education. Whereas formerly suggestions of close links were often dismissed as doctrinaire Marxist views, now there is general agreement on the reality of the relationship but differences in valuations of it, and particularly on which should be the primary determinant. A second issue, and the one given more attention here, is the nature of the relationship, and whether education and the economy interact mechanistically, or more dynamically and creatively. This issue is significant because a sound understanding of the relationship is basic to effective action in response to situations such as the current one of economic constraint.

The position from which this discussion starts finds the former interpretation unsatisfactory because, in stressing impersonal structural entities such as society, the state, the economy, the system, capitalism or socialism, and mechanistic interactions, it incidentally ascribes to people essentially passive roles in educational and other social activities. In contrast, the position taken here is that people are dynamic, creative and interpretative, and driven to pursue particular personal and group concerns — or interests to adapt a well-established concept. These interests comprise a variety of types — some personal such as to achieve competence and autonomy in different forms, some social such as to achieve identity, status, wealth and authority, and some in relation to groups, organizations and other social entities with which people associate. And one consequence, incidentally, of giving primary significance to people as sources of action, producers of strategies and constructors of organizations, ideologies, rationales and the like is that these latter are then given secondary and instrumental significance.

It is also evident that the concept of interest is not adequate by itself; necessary too are power and social justice. Power, meaning a capacity to achieve personal and group ends, even if to do so is at a cost to other people, and social justice, meaning a concern for the entitlements of others, and so restraint in the pursuit of personal or group ends out of consideration for others, are both basic elements in social activities and arrangements. For example, those with considerable power are able to achieve control of existing social arrangements or create new ones for use in the pursuit of their personal and group interests. Those arrangements then constitute the social reality to which less powerful people — typically particular ethnic minorities, women, younger and older age groups, and working and unemployed classes of people — accommodate so that it is they who have passive and accommodative roles. Concurrently, it is a sense of social justice among the more powerful that results in less coerciveness, exploitativeness or predatoriness than might otherwise be the case.

In these circumstances then the significance of economic conditions is in that they constitute a source of resources and opportunites. Hence, a period of economic growth, or of an 'expanding economic cake', is associated with a 'trickle down' of benefits such as rising standards of living, expanding and more open educational arrangements, and increased participation in schooling. In contrast, a period of economic constraint, with its reduced resources and opportunities, means efforts by the more powerful to maintain, if not continue to improve, their circumstances and achievements so that the burden of an overall economic slowdown is directed down upon the less powerful. Now because schooling is so useful as a mechanism for disadvantaging some and achieving advantages for others, we can expect it to be used increasingly as an exclusionary mechanism. And that can be achieved by such devices as increasing the rigidities of structuring in programs, class and school organization, teaching strategies, examination procedures, and so on.

For such reasons as these, the present period of economic constraint is interesting both in itself and in the more general study of education and economy relationships. In particular, we can expect a period of economic constraint to be accompanied by more intense struggles and conflicts in competitions for limited resources and opportunities, and normally less visible groups to be more apparent and more observable, so that more extensive observations and interpretations can be made.

Obviously, the general thesis regarding the relevance of econo-mic circumstances to individual and group activity can be explored in many areas of social activity and in the earlier version of this paper (Hunt, 1982) an examination of a variety of trends produced evidence to support the thesis. Here, however, attention is limited to education and, because the conservative Liberal-National Party coalition gov-erned from late 1975 until early 1983 and so had responsibility for policy during the greater proportion of the period of economic constraint, it will be the major focus of this discussion. However, a brief examination will be made of the emerging policies of the Labor government elected in March 1983. Finally, some more general issues will be considered in the concluding section.

Trends in Australian Education

Before focussing on trends in Australian education since the mid 1970s when economic growth slowed, it is useful to briefly review longer-term developments. This was done comprehensively in the Williams Report (1979, chapters 1 and 2) and a selection of data from it is adequate to show a consistent growth in educational activity. That children stayed longer at school is indicated in an increase in the attendance of 16 year-olds from approximately 22 per cent in 1957 to nearly 60 per cent in 1977, and a rise in the retention rate from first to final form of secondary schooling from 22.7 per cent in 1967 to 35.3 per cent in 1977. At the tertiary or post-secondary level, undergradu-ate enrolments rose from 4.7 per cent of the 17 to 22 year age group in 1957 to 9.5 per cent in 1977 in universities, while enrolments in colleges of advanced education or their earlier equivalents rose from 3.0 to 9.6 per cent. Concurrently, resources allocated to education rose from 2.1 per cent of GDP in 1956/57 to 5.8 per cent in 1976/77. That much of that increase was due to increased Commonwealth spending on education is evidenced by its increase from 2.6 per cent of all government spending on education in 1957 to 42.1 per cent in 1977.

Not surprisingly, this growth in educational activity was linked to a steadily growing economy. Statistics published by the Reserve Bank of Australia (1980, p.109) show that GDP rose by 19.1 per cent between 1954/55 and 1959/60, by 23.5 per cent between 1964/65 and 1969/70 and by 17.7 per cent between 1969/70 and 1974/75. Howev-er, although the period of the 1950s and 1960s may be seen as the golden age of education, clearly the mid-1970s were even more golden than elsewhen. From a position where educational expenditure constituted 3.9 per cent of GDP in 1969/70 and rose to 4.6 per cent in 1972/73, it was taken by a Labor government to 6.2 per cent by 1975/76 (ABS Cat.No.4101.0, 1980, p.110).[1] And although the increased expenditure was spread over all sectors of the educational enterprise, additional support was given to needier schools together with such groups as children of Aborigines, migrants and parents in poverty.[2] So while overall the growth in educational activity reflected the influence of factors associated with economic growth, such as greater capacity to support children at school and greater resources with which to supply schooling, it also reflected differences in ideological commitments to the education of a population.

In considering recent trends in education it is useful to begin by studying participation patterns because it is here that the effects of policies and social pressures to increase or decrease opportunities are likely to be apparent. In turn, in considering them it is useful to distinguish between two influences on participation in schooling. Given greater difficulties in obtaining employment, we can expect some decline in enthusiasm for schooling and so a trend for youth to leave earlier. However, the thesis being explored here also suggests that policies will be developed to discourage continued participation, or at least change its character, particularly at certain points. Given the general ladder-like system of schooling in Australia, we would expect the upper levels to be restricted, allowing relatively fewer people through to the more attractive opportunities. At the same time, the process of exclusion can be influenced by measures as early as primary and even pre-schooling that discourage or lower aspirations and expectations, and prospects of achieving highly in schooling.

Turning now to the data, we see that a notable feature of participation rates in recent years was their decline, particularly at the tertiary level. In fact, so significant was that decline that the Commonwealth Tertiary Education Commission (CTEC) made it the subject of a special enquiry (CTEC, 1982) and data from their report are reproduced in table 1.1. The data show a slight decline in the participation rates of male 16 year-olds in schools, a similar decline among males and a slight increase among females in the proportions of an age group continuing to the final year of secondary schooling, a slight increase among males and a substantial increase among females in technical and further education (TAFE) enrolments, and a marked decline among males and females in both universities and colleges of advanced education (CAEs).

In an accompanying paper commissioned by the CTEC, Hayden

Table 1.1: Total Education Participation Rates, by Age and Educational Sector, 1975, 1980 and 1981

Level or sector of participation		1975	1980	1981
16 year-olds in schools[a]	M	54.0	55.7	54.6
	F	52.1	57.9	57.9
	T	53.1	56.8	56.2
Apparent retention rate to	M	34.6	31.9	32.0
final year of secondary schooling[b]	F	35.3	37.3	37.8
	T	34.9	34.5	34.8
Students aged 17-21 years in	M	24.1	25.7	27.7
technical and further education[a]	F	8.7	13.0	13.3
	T	16.5	19.4	20.6
Colleges of advanced education[a]	M	5.0	4.7	4.5
	F	6.1	5.9	5.6
	T	5.5	5.3	5.1
Universities[a]	M	7.2	6.2	6.0
	F	5.0	4.7	4.7
	T	6.1	5.4	5.4

Sources:
[a] Commonwealth Tertiary Education Commission (1982) *Learning and Earning*, vol. 2, Canberra, AGPS, pp. 13–15.
[b] Commonwealth Department of Education and Youth Affairs, (1983) *Statistical Monograph no. 3*, Apparent Grade Retention Rates and Age Participation Rates, 9th edn, Canberra, Statistics Unit, September.

(1982) reviewed the literature on participation and concluded that both economic and social factors were associated with people turning away from university and social factors were associated with people turning away from university and college attendance. Economic factors included the higher cost of obtaining a higher education and lessened returns from particular qualifications, partly due to a common necessity to accept lower positions than hitherto would have been the case. Social factors included reduced parental encouragement or enthusiasm for higher education. These factors appear to have had differential significance because the decline was greater among young males, and youth from rural and lower socio-economic backgrounds. Curiously, however, while Hayden noted government discouragement of participation in higher education (p. 152) he did not include it as a major factor in his summary (p. 154). Because of the thesis argued in this chapter, that aspect will be explored further here, first in more concrete terms, and subsequently in terms of orientations and attitudes.

A major expression of a government's commitments and priorities is in its expenditure programs, although certain features of these need to be well understood. For example, commitments develop over time, and are difficult to change in the short term. Consequently, key indicators may be more evident in changes in relativities, in 'fine tuning' adjustments, or in small-scale innovations or in the selection of or modifications to programs. In addition, Commonwealth activity has been characterized by an illuminating interaction between the government and its education commissions, particularly the Schools Commission. Established by the former Labor government to identify needs of schools and differentiate between them in recommending support, that preoccupation clashed with the succeeding coalition government's predisposition to support by per capita grants that ignore differing circumstances of families and schools and so favour the more affluent. In consequence, the government not only closely directed its working through the issuance of guidelines but also made important changes to its membership.

One common measure of commitment of resources is educational expenditure as a percentage of gross domestic product (GDP). That proportion increased to peak at 6.4 per cent in 1977/78 and has since declined (ABS Cat. No. 4101.0, (1980) p. 110). However the significance of those trends is substantially effected by changing enrolments and so a more useful indicator is expenditure per student. On that point, Burke (1983), reviewing expenditure in the 1970s and 1980s, notes substantial increases over the five years to 1980/81, but he also notes in respect of higher education that a proportion of increased costs are due to higher salaries for an ageing, more senior staff, together with higher superannuation and other payments as those arrangements have been more generously funded. Hence an increase in costs per student does not necessarily mean improvements in the quality of education.

A second area in which to explore priorities and commitments is in changes in expenditure patterns. Data on more recent trends are provided in reports of the Commonwealth education commissions and in the statements of guidelines to those commissions. Table 1.2 reports actual spending for the years 1976, 1979 and 1982 which span the coalition parties' period of government, and proposed spending for 1984, which is the first full year for the Labor party. From table 1.2 it can be seen that for the period of government by the coalition parties the major proportion of school reductions were recurrent

Table 1.2: Recent Trends in Commonwealth Expenditure on Education

Program	1976	1979	1982	1984
Govenment schools				
Recurrent general support	31.7	28.5	26.0	24.1
migrant education	3.2	3.0	4.2[a]	3.9[a]
disadvantaged schools	2.9	2.7	2.5	2.2
special schools	1.8	1.8	1.8	1.6
participation and equity				3.1
computer education				0.4
Capital	22.1	20.4	12.1	12.0
Non-government schools				
Recurrent general support	27.4	32.5	42.6	43.0
migrant education	1.2	1.2	1.6[a]	1.4[a]
disadvantaged schools	0.5	0.4	0.4	0.4
special schools	0.6	0.5	0.5	0.4
short term emergency				
assistance	0.0	0.1	0.1	—
participation and equity				0.4
computer education				0.1
Capital	4.5	4.8	4.3	4.1
Joint Programs	4.2	4.1	3.6	2.9
Total on schools	100.0	100.0	100.0	100.0
Universities	54.4	54.1)		87.2
		)	89.0	
Colleges	38.8	36.6)		
TAFE	6.8	9.3	11.0	12.8
Total on post-secondary education	100.0	100.0	100.0	100.0

Note:
[a] Now English as a second language.
Sources:
Schools, 1976 and 1979: (1979) *Australian Students and Their Schools*, Canberra, Schools Commission.
Universities and colleges, 1976 and 1979: Tertiary Education Commission, (1981) *Report for 1982–84 Triennium*, vol. 1, pt. 1, Canberra, AGPS, p. 261.
1982 allocations: Commonwealth Schools Commission, (1982) *Triennium 1982–84, Report for 1983*, Canberra, Commonwealth Publishing and Printing Co., August, p. 34; and Commonwealth Tertiary Education Commission, (1982) *Report for the 1982–84 Triennium*, vol. 3, recommendations for 1983, Canberra, APGS, August, p. 5.
1984 proposal allocations: Commonwealth Schools Commission Guidelines, Canberra, p. 31; and Commonwealth Tertiary Education Commission Guidelines, (1983) Canberra, (mimeo), July, p. 15.

general support and capital funding for government schools, while the major increases were in the recurrent general support for non-government schools. These trends become more significant, however, when more specific changes are considered. One was a growing emphasis on transition programs, justified as necessary to prepare youth for employment, and which were financed partly by switching funds from general to specific grants, thus reducing options available to state education departments. A second shift was in the rearrangement of support between different categories of non-government schools; whereas the Karmel Report (1973, p. 87) recommended eight categories of schools for funding purposes and the phasing out of grants for the more affluent by 1976, subsequent Commonwealth actions reduced the categories to three, and the coalition government assured the top group of grants at the rate of 20 per cent of average government school costs. Moreover, the schools with least resources were to receive only twice the amount granted to wealthier schools by 1983. Further, in that payments were made relative to student enrolments they ignored the different circumstances of parents and, reflecting differential attendance, favoured schools that attracted students with greater staying power. This tendency to favour the more affluent was no chance event; it was recognized as early in the coalition government's regime as between 1976 and 1978 by Scotton (1980, pp. 12–13) but it was also a characteristic thrust of successive coalition government policies for schools since the early 1960s.

In the post-secondary sector, the data show a steady reduction in relative support for universities and colleges, and modest growth for TAFE. In addition, other measures, such as a proposal to introduce fees for postgraduate students, prospective rather than retrospective budgeting for increased costs, the development of centres of excellence by redistributing general university resources, thereby reducing the resources available to unselected sectors of universities, further constrained and even directed institutional functioning.

Finally, support for student and other types of activity for youth was steadily reduced. The CTEC (1982) report examined data on the issue and found that while the Consumer Price Index moved from 100.0 in 1974 to 237.1 by March 1982, tertiary education allowances moved to 197 for students living at home, and to 184.5 for those living away from home, while unemployment benefits for those 17 years and younger moved to only 138.5, and benefits for those 18 years and over moved to 223.5 (vol. 2, p. 45). Thus for youth not in the workforce, support was steadily reduced relative to the cost of living.

Taking these policies together, we can postulate a pattern to which the educational system as a whole was directed. Publicly operated schools and the particular groups of children who attend them were given a lesser priority. Concurrently, more generous funding of privately operated schools, particularly those serving the more affluent sectors of the population, enabled them to provide better services and compete more effectively for tertiary entrance and so for access to higher level professional and executive positions and opportunities. Beyond schooling limitation of university and college activity, and particularly the former, limited the proportion of the population that could qualify for attractive opportunities and statuses, and gain other advantages of education, while concurrent expansion of TAFE at a lower level served partly at least as a mechanism for lowering aspirations and expectations of large proportions of students, and for deflecting them into sub-professional and other lower level occupations and positions.

The Articulation of National Policy

The determination of goals, establishing their relative priority, and the planning, justification and undertaking of relevant courses of action requires careful coordination, expression and execution — that is, articulation — if they are to be effectively performed. At the national level of action, relatively little of this is directly observable, and much of that which is observable is also consciously presented as part of a strategy for influencing action and reaction. Partly for that reason, the media are a major source of data of that which is observable and interpretable. However, the many channels or mediums, the extensive amount of material which they transmit, and the sheer mass of material that accumulates, makes a comprehensive examination and interpretation quite impossible. The compromise adopted here has been to examine material transmitted through a particular section of the media, namely, a selection of several major newspapers. I would argue that in such a source will be found at least references to the main aspects of the articulation of national policies. I have surveyed the period from 1975 to the present.

As has been indicated, late 1975 constitutes a watershed in the activities of national government with constraint of schooling, notably through financial provision, a key element of the coalition government's program. However, a necessity to constrain was argued earlier, not only in the persistent advocacy by the then opposition and other interest groups and their spokespeople, but also by the Labor government during its last year in office (*Australian*, 13 May 1975; *Sun*, 23 September 1975).

The subsequent actions of the coalition government involved generally a decreasing rate of increase, including actual cuts in some sectors, and changes in priorities. Even so, the cuts were not so severe as in other societies such as the United Kingdom, and so less than they might have been or as some would have liked them to be.

What might be termed the groundswell for constraint and reorientation of schooling was generated by a number of individuals and groups of broadly conservative stance, including an element of 'new conservatism' (*Bulletin*, 18 April 1978 and 6 November 1979). The proponents were mainly employer and industry groups and their spokespeople, together with some traditionalist educationists. Employers and producers sought a differentially competent and graded workforce, and looked to schools to teach basic skills and attitudes of compliancy, and to sift and sort children (*Sun*, 3 August 1976; *Age*, 13 September 1976, 23 September 1967 and 14 December 1978). The educationists shared a commitment to basic skills and a teaching process that incidentally produced a graded school population (*Australian*, 8 September 1975 and 24 April 1978; *Herald*, 6 April 1976), but some also upheld a cultural-educative role for schooling (*Australian*, 2 September 1975; *Age*, 24 April 1978). These differences between educationists and employer-producers caused no problem, however, because both could be accommodated by selective elite schools for high performers who incidentally provide leadership in the future. The several groups were on common ground again in a lack of concern for the experiences and prospects of the lesser performers who, again incidentally, are available to perform the more menial tasks in a society.

At the tertiary level criticism was in terms of overproduction of graduates generally, or in this or that field, with concurrent arguments for the extension of technical and further education, and the reduction of the university and college sectors of tertiary education (*Australian*, 26 June 1975; *Courier Mail*, 28 October 1975; *Age*, 30 December 1976). It is ironic that while the functioning of the economy was used to justify reorientation in tertiary education, and thereby reduce the production of more specialized graduates, its incapacity to provide employment for youth at lower levels of competence was only infrequently acknowledged by the critics; rather, blame was laid on the schools and those who worked in them. Thus both thrusts of criticism justified action to constrain and reorient the whole system of education to vocationalism, while the economy was the unappraised and unblamed 'sacred cow'.

Concurrently, these beliefs and interpretations found ready and strong support with leaders of the government. Deputy Prime Minister Anthony was early quoted as warning parents to be watchful of the political teaching of some teachers and to organize to counter their efforts (*Sun*, 1 December 1975). Prime Minister Fraser also early emphasized the link between schooling and unemployment, and the establishment of the Williams Committee to enquire into education, training and employment, presented as the most substantial review since the Martin Committee's examination of tertiary education in the early 1960s, was specifically 'to explore the role of the educational system in preparing people for work' (*Education News*, 1976, p. 52). In the event the Williams Committee neither indicted schooling nor quietened the critics; the Prime Minister and others continued to castigate schooling (*Sun*, 9 April 1979; *Age*, 15 January 1980; *Financial Review*, 21 October 1980). However, the basis of criticism broadened to include a concern about the academic bias of school programs and the neglect of some 70 or more per cent of 'non-academic' children (*Herald*, 3 October 1979; *Australian*, 26 August 1980), taking advantage of a thread of argument that had been building up at least since a school-to-work transition report of 1976 (Department of Education, 1976). At the same time, the thrust to provide more practical or less academic programs for the lesser performers had a touch of bitter irony; it occurred when employment was becoming an idle hope for many youths, and in contrast with the quite different kinds of programs proposed by quite different critics who advocated education for living, for self-expression and personal development, and for fostering a more humane society (Schools Commission, 1980).

Concurrently and complementarily, the national government also promoted job-oriented programs that supplemented schooling (*Financial Review*, 23 September 1976; *Age*, 20 November 1976). These took many forms and were of uncertain effectiveness, with achievements only recently coming under systematic appraisal. While they have, of course, been held to express concern for the circumstances and prospects of youth, they were also seen as devices for reducing the incidence of registered unemployed and, in the circumstances of a shortage of jobs, as changing nothing other than the order of youth in the queues seeking employment.

A further thrust in respect of schooling that had considerable potential influence on the functioning of schooling, particularly in relation to the moves noted above, was for a wider range of examinations at several points of leaving schooling (*Age*, 29 September 1976 and 8 May 1980; *Australian*, 8 November 1978). The argument for this was again provided by employers and traditionalist educationists, although for different reasons. They were also joined by some practising educational specialists who may have acted from a definite philosophical position or been technocrats keen to practise particular skills, or who discerned a prevailing orientation and saw a prospect of achieving a rewarding career. The significance to schooling of a wider range of examinations is, as has been noted, considerable. Inevitably it seems (and probably due to pressures from the expectations of employers, parents and students who seek to maximize their prospects within the established circumstances and structures) schools adapt to meet such realities. And invariably a consequence is the grouping of students by their assumed prospects into either differentiated schools or programs or both, with profound consequences for the different levels of performers, regardless of their overall competence, as Lacey (1970) showed so clearly in his study of students in a streamed grammar school. Inevitably, of course, such developments lower expectations of many students and increase the exclusionary role of schooling.

Still another thrust of national concern was the preparation of teachers. Critics nominated both their technical competence and their ideological or philosophical bases as sources of their inadequacies (*Age*, 3 July 1976; *Australian*, 17 November 1976 and 12 December 1978). The absence of 'over time' data, or even assertions in contradiction of such data as do exist, did not deter the critics nor even cause them to qualify their assertions. Indeed, the persistence with descriptions of the characteristics and performances of teachers, despite a lack of evidence, and ultimately the offering of interpretations and solutions to problems which had not been established as existing, testified to a straightforward political-ideological attack that was waged on schooling, and on the educators who were its more visible practitioners. Not surprisingly, the critics were spokespeople from the same groups as identified in respect of schooling generally.

Not surprisingly, again, the issue of teacher preparation was also taken up by national government as one for examination, leading to the setting up of the Auchmuty Committee (*Education News*, 1978, p. 39). It was established to review teacher education and possibly expose its culpability. In the event, the Auchmuty Report (1980) also failed to oblige, and actually went on to emphasize the problems of teachers in maintaining their adequacy in changing circumstances, and recommend study leave and in-service programs. However, government did not take up such recommendations; rather, conditions of employment were restricted, with increased use of short-term and temporary contracts, and so of longer periods of trial before tenured appointments were made. Further, the introduction of staffing ceilings gave some indication of worsening staff-student ratios.

The Labor Alternative

In appraising the significance of Labor as an alternative government it is important to recall that it has been in power nationally only since March 1983. Nonetheless it has had opportunities in its first budget and elsewhere to establish particular priorities and strategies.

Budgetary decisions indicate it is emerging as modestly redistributive rather than expansionary, planning to improve the schooling circumstances of most children relative to those attending more affluent private schools. Labor also plans to re-establish the Curriculum Development Centre (CDC)as a national support agency, but located now within the Schools Commission. It is also directing special attention to particular groups such as early leavers, and planning a modest expansion of tertiary education (Guidelines, 1983).

Of considerable significance too, is the positive tone adopted towards publicly operated education. The Minister for Education has repeatedly expressed support for all sections of the system of educational institutions (for example, *Australian*, 23 March 1983; *School Bell*, 1983). Of considerable significance, too, is the interest, articulated especially by the Minister for Science and Technology, in promoting technological competence and innovation in Australia (*Australian*, 6 May 1983 and 10 August 1983). Altogether, there appears to be firm support for a more educated and competent populace.

In appraising Labor as a force in education, it is also relevant to take account of developments at state levels where Labor has governed in New South Wales since 1977 and replaced Liberal or coalition party governments in three other states between May 1982 and February 1983. Of these latter, the one in Victoria has had longest in power, including two budgets in which to implement its policies. It too is showing a strong commitment to publicly operated schooling, emphasizing need in allocations to privately operated schools, and proposing to devolve considerable authority to regions and schools, thus fostering participation in a broader than demographic sense of that process. And recently, too, the longer standing NSW Labor government is also breaking with traditional funding practices and giving priority to need among private schools (APC Review, 1983, p. 5).

Despite these distinctive policy thrusts, there remain some important similarities between the two sets of parties. For example, although several state Labor governments have initiated devolutionary moves, they continue to support the operation of key control mechanisms such as centralized funding, staffing and examinations at the end of secondary schooling. These last effectively bring uniformity to a substantial proportion of senior secondary school programs. Again, while some emphasize need among privately operated schools, their support for comparable publicly operated schools in every community essentially ignores substantial differences between students in their circumstances and leaves those of better-off parents substantially ahead of children of poorer parents. That support of the status quo is increased by the practice of spending more per student at higher levels of schooling, which are more commonly attended by children of the more affluent. As a consequence students who go on to take out a degree, and who are usually from more affluent families, have up to three times as much public funds spent on them as children who leave school at the minimum age of 15 years (Schools Commission, 1981, pp. 43–4).

These orientations are not surprising, however, when we examine the background to Labor party policy making. For example, it is evident that a major source of Labor support, the Australian Council of Trade Unions (ACTU), has been substantially transformed over recent years, with a considerable infusion of white collar, technical and professional groups (Hand, 1981). A corollary of that development is that ACTU policies on education have been substantially prepared by members of educational employee groups so that they are very much industrial statements, whatever their educational merits may be.

While it is not apparent that Labor party policies have been written on the same basis, it is evident that teacher organizations have strongly supported the Labor party in electoral campaigns, and that many teachers have won seats as party members (for example, *Geelong Advertiser*, 8 March 1983; *Age*, 29 October 1983). Accordingly, current or former teachers participate in formulating Labor policies, and in implementing them when in government and, in doing so, work from assumptions that substantially endorse important features of present arrangements such as a state systems of schools, treasury funding of departments and schools, departmental staffing of schools, hierarchical career structures, comparable schools in every community, and increased expenditure at higher levels of education. Certainly Labor policies are substantially closer to the policies of teachers than other organizations.

More generally, however, it is arguable that Labor policies on education are more compatible with the interests of a middle sector of operatives in Australian society than they are with the traditional working class of blue collar workers, particularly the less skilled and poorer elements of that sector. Certainly, the power or influence of the former with the Labor party could well lie in their marginal status as transient voters who switch from one party to another, together with their political skills and competencies in exercising influence in social and political activities.

Discussion

The distinctive styles of the different national and, to some extent, state governments in Australia indicate that they mediate the impact of changing economic circumstances on areas of activity such as education. However, while governments are entities in their own rights, with concerns such as to stay in power constituting distinctive interests, they also have constituencies and affiliations with particular groups or sectors of society, and it is necessary to examine these in order to fully understand differences between policies. Then, for example, we can see that the coalition parties clearly relate to groups with property and commercial interests and who are able to employ the more individualistic goal-attaining strategies and uphold a commitment to entrepreneurial styles that economic resources allow, and which are exemplified in the working of the market place. In contrast, the Labor party clearly relates to the workforce, although increasingly to technocratic-bureaucratic operatives and, having a base in knowledge and skills, employs strategies that emphasize rights to share goods and services and to enjoy achievements and benefits, and generate a necessity to organize, achieve legitimacy or authority, and take collective action, as is exemplified in the forum. However, neither preoccupation implies a neglect of alternative modes of operating; the difference is more one of primacy of orientation with alternatives used complementarily with the major strategies.

The significance of the economy also means that both sets of groups have been substantially affected as Australia has increasingly become part of a world economy, and in which it operates as a minor to modest entity, with major power and decision-making centres located elsewhere. As a consequence, those guided primarily by economic criteria sometimes find themselves pre-empted or constrained by policies and strategies formulated elsewhere. In contrast, those who uphold claims for sharing resources and opportunities also find it necessary if not useful to uphold basic rights for all, and to give a higher priority to essentially Australian pre-occupations, and seek to contest the dominance of international power centres.

From the more obvious groupings it is relatively easy to arrive at interpretations that emphasize polarized positions, thereby producing and sustaining conceptions that are more formed and dichotomized than exist in reality. At the same time, it is also easy to give considerable significance to individualism and opportunism and see social arrangements as inherently unstable because of the thrust of self-seeking predatoriness. Each of these more extreme and simplistic interpretations is unsound in that the first neglects individualism and the second neglects power, compassion and other elements of social binding. It is that range of human attributes that make alternative forms of social arrangements possible, and give significance to circumstances and to exceptional people who can foster an emphasis of one line of action or another. But basic are enduring human attributes which allow prospects that the current constrained economic circumstances are bringing into clearer form in Australia and in other societies.

Notes

1 Presumably a correction has been made to the figure given in the Williams Report and quoted earlier.
2 Developments in education under the national Labor government of 1972–75 have been summarized by Ferber (1978) and discussed by Davey (1978) and will not be considered in detail here.

References

Apc Review (1983) *The 'Me-Too' Bandwagon*, 9, 3.
Auchmuty Report (1980) *Report of the National Inquiry into Teacher Education*, Canberra, AGPS.
Australian Bureau of Statistics (1980) *Social Indicators*, 3, Canberra,

ABS, Cat. no. 4101.0.

BURKE, G. (1983) 'Public educational expenditure in the seventies and eighties', *Australian Economic Review*, 63, third quarter, pp. 34–35.

CTEC (1982) *Learning and Earning*, 2 vols, Canberra, AGPS.

DAVEY, P. (1978) 'Financing of education' in SCOTTON, R.B. and FERBER, H. (Eds) *Public Expenditures and Social Policy in Australia,* vol. 1, The Whitlam Years, 1972–75, Melbourne, Longman Cheshire.

DEPARTMENT OF EDUCATION (1976) *Transition from School to Work or Further Study,* Canberra, Department of Education.

EDUCATION NEWS (1976) *Committee of Inquiry into Education and Training — The Prime Minister's Statement,* 15, 11 and 12 (double issue) p. 52.

EDUCATION NEWS (1975) *National Inquiry into Teacher Education: Terms of Reference,* 16, 6, p. 39.

FERBER, H. (1978) 'Diary of legislative and administrative changes' in SCOTTON, R.B. and FERBER, H. (Eds) *Public Expenditures and Social Policy in Australia*, vol. 1, The Whitlam Years, 1972–75, Melbourne, Longman Cheshire.

GUIDELINES (1983) *Commonwealth Schools Commission Guidelines and Commonwealth Tertiary Education Commission Guidelines,* Canberra, mimeo, July.

HALL, R. (1981) 'FAUSA and the ACTU: The case for affiliation', *Vestes*, 24, 1, pp. 31–6.

HAYDEN, M. (1982) 'Factors affecting participation by young people in tertiary education: A review of recent Australian literature and research', in CTEC *Learning and Earning*, vol. 2, Canberra, AGPS.

HUNT, F.J. (1982) 'Education and the constrained economy', *The British Journal of Sociology of Education*, 3, pp. 235–48.

KARMEL REPORT (1983) *Schools in Australia*, Report of the Interim Committee for the Australian Schools Commission, Canberra, Schools Commission.

LACEY, C. (1970) *Hightown Grammar,* Manchester, Manchester University Press.

RESERVE BANK OF AUSTRALIA (1980) *Australian Economic Statistics, 1949–50 to 1978–79,* 1, tables, occasional paper no 8A, Sydney, Reserve Bank of Australia.

SCHOOLS COMMISSION (1980) *Schooling for 15 to 16 year olds,* Canberra, Schools Commission.

SCHOOLS COMMISSION (1981) *Report for the Triennium 1982–84,* Canberra, AGPS.

SCOTTON, R.B. (1980) 'The Fraser government and social expenditures', in SCOTTON, R.B. and FERBER, H. (Eds) *Public Expenditures and Social Policy in Australaia,* Vol. II, The First Fraser Years, 1976–78, Melbourne, Longman Cheshire.

SCOTTON, R.B. and FERBER, H. (Eds) (1978) *Public Expenditures and Social Policy in Australia,* vol. 1, The Whitlam Years, 1972–75, Melbourne, Longman Cheshire.

SCOTTON, R.B. and FERBER, H. (Eds) (1980) *Public Expenditures and Social Policy in Australia,* Vol. II, The First Fraser Years, 1976–78, Mel-

bourne, Longman Cheshire.
Tertiary Education Commission (1981) *Report for 1982-84 Triennium*, vol. 1, part 1, Canberra, AGPS.
Williams Report (1979) *Education, Training and Employment*, Report of the Committee of Inquiry into Education and Training, vol. 1, Canberra, AGPS.

Newspapers

Age

'Professor takes cane to teachers', 3 July 1976
'Students lack work ethic, say employers', 13 September 1976
'School's out, now to learn', 23 September 1976
'Bring back exams', 29 September 1976
'More leavers to get job subsidy', 20 November 1976
'Graduates face a 5000 job shortfall', 30 December 1976
'Academic study isn't just work training', 24 April 1978
'Education is blamed', 14 December 1978
'PM slams schools for youth job problems', 15 January 1980
'"Bring back external exams", says professor', 8 May 1980
'The teachers have a lot to learn', 29 October 1983

Australian

'Hint of possible education cuts', 13 May 1975
'Job market swamped by graduates', 26 June 1975
'Foreign languages drift causes culture crisis', 2 September 1975
'Schools must get back to the three R's', 8 September 1975
'Scandal in schooling: they're not taught to teach English', 17 November 1976
'Education tyranny — Messel', 24 April 1978
'Education slammed', 8 November 1978
'Bjelke cracks down on sloppy teachers', 12 December 1978
'PM blames system of education for job problems of young', 26 August 1980

'Ryan tips modest growth if institutions fit govt aims', 23 March 1983

'"Sunrise" technology an urgent priority', 6 May 1983

'The need for innovation', 10 August 1983

Bulletin 'Capitalism becoming respectable', 18 April 1978

'The growing voice of the academic right', 6 November 1979

Courier Mail 'Jobs may be hard for graduates', 28 October 1975

Financial Review 'School leavers job scheme', 23 September 1976

'Education blamed for lack of skills in trades', 21 October 1980

Geelong Advertiser 'They're a learned lot', 8 March 1983

Herald 'Head backs three R's', 6 April 1976

'Education get rap from PM', 3 October 1979

School Bell 'A ten-point plan for better education', August 1983

Sun 'That's it! Hayden: We've got to the limit', 23 September 1975

'Anthony raps "bias" in class', 1 December 1975

'Firms rap school system', 3 August 1976

'Schools "neglect job role"', 9 April 1979

2 Canada: Educational Policy-Making: Impacts of the 1980s Recession

Thomas R. Williams
Queen's University, Kingston,
Ontario, Canada

As this chapter was being written, in the spring of 1984, Canada was struggling to emerge from the worst recession since the Great Depression. Clearly, the booming economic times of the 1960s and early 1970s are over. The previously predictable, ever increasing, rate of growth of spending on many social services, particularly education, has stopped. Given the facts that all levels of government are now constrained by large debt loads and that the economic climate has seriously curtailed government revenue expectations, no one expects significant increases in government expenditures for social services in the near future. Indeed, some of yesterday's 'sacred cows', such as education, have begun to lose their untouchable status. In a recent review conducted by Canada's leading financial newspaper (the *Financial Post*) it was noted,

> Education, in particular should receive relatively less, as school enrolment falls. Health care will have to accommodate increasing numbers of elderly people as the population ages, but will have few extra resources to do so. (Harris, 1983, p. 32)

During the recent recession, the traditionally stable environment in which educational policies in Canada have been formulated, experienced major upheavals. Double digit inflation became a fact of life reaching 12.5 per cent in 1981/82. Interest rates reached almost 22 per cent in 1982 driving unprecedented numbers of businesses into bankruptcy and exacerbating government debt loads. Unemployment increased by 55 per cent in the four-year period from 1980 until

1984 (vs 40 per cent in the United States). The adjusted unemployment rate jumped from 7.5 per cent in 1981 to between 11 and 12 per cent in 1983. It is estimated that approximately 600,000 jobs were lost during the recession and current projections suggest that even by 1989, the unemployment rate will have dropped only to 9 per cent — a substantial increase over the rate at the beginning of this decade. A combination of factors has resulted in a disproportionate impact on the 15 to 24 year-old age group where unemployment rose from 13.2 per cent in 1980 to 18.18 per cent in 1982. 'These factors included economic stagnation, a rapid increase in the number of entrants into the labour force as the baby boom generation attained school leaving age and a rapid increase in female participation' (Brown, 1983, p. 15).

It should not be particularly surprising in this climate, which saw tremendous numbers of workers in the private sector unemployed, that those employed in the public sector started to be seen by both business and government interests as fair game for retrenchment initiatives. This change in perspective has had a shattering impact on the traditionally 'sacred' status of public sector workers, including members of the education community.

Selected Determinants of Canadian Educational Policy

Educational policy in Canada is developed within a federal system. Historically, the official role of the federal government relative to school affairs has been minimal. For instance, the 1975 *OECD Report* notes, 'Officially, there is *no* Federal presence in the area of educational policy, and the Federal govenment behaves (at least in public) as if there were none' (Organization for Economic Cooperation and Development, 1975, p. 16). The apparent contradiction to this observation is the fact that the federal government does contribute substantial financial resources to elementary and secondary education (in excess of $424 m in 1980/81) and it exercises a significant steering effect on some decisions affecting educational policy, i.e. wage limitations, the reduction of regional disparities in educational expenditures and employment training programs. The relationship between the federal government, which constitutionally assigns responsibility for the governance of education to each of Canada's ten provinces, is a contentious accommodation, characterized '... largely by avoidance of open political debate and by relatively closed and informal negotiations among politicians and government officials' (Lucas, 1977, p. 14).

The most powerful players in the determination of educational policies in Canada are the ten provincial governments. They supply approximately two-thirds of the revenues for elementary and secondary education and determine most of the significant parameters under which both local school boards and post-secondary institutions operate. The Canadian political culture and traditions heavily weight the relationship between provincial and local governments towards the provinces. There is a long tradition of strong provincial interventions on educational matters. Ironically, within the centralized tradition, the 1960s and 1970s also saw local school boards in Canada operating in a more fiscally independent fashion from municipal governments and their constituents than in other western democracies. The overall relationship between the provinces and local boards of education, while very centralized relative to the American pattern, underwent a substantial decentralization period in the 1970s relative to Canadian operating experiences. Vis-à-vis the provinces, local boards became more active in the determination of policies dealing with personnel and program and, to a more limited extent, budgets. As will be noted later, events associated with the recession and demographic changes have dramatically reversed the decentralist trend.

Traditionally, at both the provincial and local levels, professional educators (including Ministry or Department of Education civil servants) have played the dominant role in the formation of educational policy. The late 1970s saw elected officials such as ministers of education and local school trustees gradually increasing their power. The rancorous, public airing of disagreements concerning educational issues began to increase in the 1970s resulting in a dramatic increase in the involvement of interest groups in the policy-making process (Williams, 1977).

A persistent Canadian problem stems from the extreme diversity among the country's regions. There have always been considerable interprovincial differences in both provincial and local government revenue per capita (reflecting the widely different industrial and resource bases of the ten provinces). The Federal government has, since the early 1970s, attempted to reduce interprovincial revenue disparities through legislative arrangements such as the Federal-Provincial Fiscal Arrangements Act. This legislation was renegotiated in the midst of the 1982 recession. Brown (1983) argues that there has been a substantial reduction in the movement toward greater equality of interprovincial differences in amounts spent per pupil enrolled in public elementary and secondary schools since the mid-1970s (pp.

14–15). A major factor in the growing inequality between provinces in the late 1970s was the very rapid economic development of western Canada due to natural resource (oil) exploitation, while other less resource rich regions of the country were unable to participate in this economic growth. However, as the recession has taken its toll, the federal government has been both unable and unwilling to maintain its equalization efforts at the early 1970 levels.

A final financial shift which has developed in the last decade has been a change in the mix of government spending devoted to social services. Health and social welfare expenditures have gained both as a percentage of government expenditures and as a percentage of GNP *at the expense of education*. While this trend was most obvious in 1970/75 and there was little change between 1975 and 1980, available evidence suggests that the percentage share of education has decreased since 1980 and the social service share has increased. This trend is partly due to demographic factors and partly due to the declining priority assigned to education during the recession. For some time, Canada has ranked very high in terms of a national commitment to education. For instance, in 1980, Canada spent 7.3 per cent of its Gross National Product on education — a commitment less than only Norway, Sweden and the Netherlands (Organization for Economic and Cooperative Development, 1983, p. 28). The percentage of GNP related to school board expenditures has decreased from 4.9 per cent in 1977 to 4.2 per cent in 1981.

Unlike other western countries such as the United States, Canada has not experienced a large number of fault finding studies of education related to the preparation of students in basic educational skills. While there have been intermittent criticisms in the media, the number of such criticisms has not, in this writer's judgment, shown a significant increase during, or immediately following, the recession. Individual provinces have conducted their own reviews, solicited briefs from interested parties and made changes in curricula which reflect a clear national trend back to the basics and increased vocationalism. While there has been some concern for several years over student competence in mathematics and language use, these concerns have not significantly altered during the recession and educators have successfully ameliorated most of these through the judicious publication of balancing sets of data.

More recently, the media have begun to raise provocative questions concerning the degree of public support for the nation's schools. (This has increased following the release of the 'excellence' studies in the United States.) For instance, a recent national survey, commissioned by the *Toronto Star* concluded that Canadians do not believe the schools are teaching students essential skills (Goldfarb, 1984, p. 1).

Isolated statements which question the heretofore unquestioned assumption that investment in education is an investment in national productivity and national welfare are also beginning to emerge. Given the horrific drops in productivity, GNP and the increases in unemployment, particularly in the 18–24 age group, some critics are now calling into question the assumption that 'the country can never spend too much on education'. With increasing frequency, Canadians are having it publicly called to their attention that, '... The optimistic estimates about the benefits of expanded expenditure upon education have not been vindicated, although education spending has increased with almost fanatical energy' (Carrigan, 1983). Criticisms such as these are then juxtaposed against the nation's unemployment rates, weak secondary industries and the uncompetitive state of the resource industries. For instance, a recent Ontario government budget paper argued that a higher quality education system was required for the sake of the province's trading position (Ontario, 1984).

Publicly, Canada's post-secondary institutions have been far more active in combatting these criticisms than elementary and secondary schools, although of late, teachers' organizations too, have marshalled data in the form of reports to present the 'real facts' to the public. Interestingly, these responses of the educational community to the growing criticisms have received little public exposure in the major media. Meanwhile the number of critical statements by politicians, members of the corporate community, science and technology interests and newspaper editors and columnists continues to increase.

Selected Impacts of the Recession on Educational Policy-Making

Several dramatic impacts on the character of the policy-making process in Canadian education are attributable to the recession. Those to be discussed in this section include: (i) a decline in the status accorded to education and educators; (ii) an increase in the influence and control of elected educational officials; (iii) a recentralization of policy-making control and direction at the provincial level of government at the expense of local school board autonomy; and (iv) an altered balance between the federal and provincial levels of government with reference to educational matters.

Changes in Status or Priority

A number of changes have occurred in the educational policy-making process in Canada during the recession which suggest that the *status* or *priority* of education has been significantly altered. The evidence of this status change is reflected in (a) changes which have occurred in actions affecting educational personnel; and (b) changes in program which have been implemented over significant objections from the elementary and secondary education community. Both of these sets of changes had financial causes rooted in the recession.

As was suggested earlier in this chapter, those engaged in public service employment have seen their traditional status eroded drastically. As the recession increased in severity, educators with their traditions of tenure and job security and with their increased profile due to a period of increased militancy during the 1970s, became more and more visible and vulnerable as having a protected status significantly 'different' from the rest of the working population. A rash of teacher strikes in the 1970s and early 1980s had raised the ire of large numbers of an otherwise dormant public. The growing militancy of some provincial teachers' groups, notably those in Quebec and British Columbia, where direct challenges to the government took place, eroded the historical status of teachers. The recession, when it hit with its dramatic impact on government revenues, sent provincial governments scurrying to find large expenditure pools to shrink which would not cause undue public or political backlash. The lever for moving on education employees was indirectly provided by the federal government.

The federal government's wage restraint program, announced in June 1982, imposed strict wage and salary controls on the federal public sector. Provinces, which supply the lion's share of education expenditures, were urged to follow suit and most did, some with a vengeance! The larger provincial governments, Ontario, British Columbia and Quebec, announced public service restraint measures which not only limited increases for teachers but also dramatically curtailed teachers' bargaining rights and their rights to strike. In fact, the Quebec provincial government went so far as to roll back wage agreements already negotiated! More recently, the British Columbia provincial government has embarked on a massive program of restraint involving the firing of large numbers of civil servants, significant decreases to school board budgets, increased control of pupil-teacher ratios, and the elimination of large numbers of teacher jobs, some in mid-year.

These changes have been accomplished with surprisingly little public outcry from non-educators concerning potential impacts on individual school systems. In fact, a public opinion survey taken in 1982, following the Quebec government's tough action to control public sector salaries, mandate working conditions and legislate 100,000 teachers back to work, revealed that while the popularity of the provincial government was then at an all time low, '. . . this same government seems to have popular support for its position in negotiating with teachers'. (Michaud, 1983, p. 63). Similarly, in British Columbia where the government stood for re-election in the middle of the recession on a platform of continued restraint of spending in the public sector (including education) and despite teacher organization efforts to influence public opinion to the contrary, the government received a new mandate of a much wider margin than even its most optimistic supporters would have predicted! Finally, a recent national survey found '. . . a growing level of public dissatisfaction with the public school system and with the teachers in it'. The author concluded, 'During the past twenty years, teachers have declined in public esteem more than any group in [Canadian] society' (Goldfarb, 1984, p. 11). Clearly, the perceived status of educators as a political influence group, has plummeted.

Increases in the Role of Elected Politicians at the Provincial Level

The apparent drop in public support for the arguments or proposals of educators on education matters is also being reflected in a decrease in the traditional influence of educators on changes to educational programs. As the recession deepened and the Canadian economy ground to a virtual halt, pressures from the business community (particularly the high technology sector) for the schools to provide 'better trained manpower' for employment in the private sector increased. During the recession it became more publicly clear that Canada's productivity record could not compare with that of other technologically advanced countries such as Japan. Hence, there has been growing pressure on school systems, particularly at the provincial policy level, for increased vocationalism, science and technology, basics and standards. As a result of these concerns, several provinces began to consider (on the direction and initiative of the ministers of education and *not* the professional civil servants in ministries of education) ways in which standards could be 'improved.' It is significant that these considerations of changes in the direction of educational policies both originated in, and were pursued from, the political arena and not, as tradition would have it, through professional bureaucratic routes.

Despite the lobbying efforts of teachers, several provinces have introduced revised curricula which limit the freedom of student choice of subjects which characterized the 1970s. Others are rapidly moving toward the compulsory introduction of technology related courses. Several have reintroduced compulsory, central examinations in an effort to control grade inflation and to 'ensure standards'. While policies such as these were discussed sporadically prior to the recession, the major variable precipitating these changes was the 'sour' economy which allowed the issues of program and standards, relative to national economic goals and performance, to be raised as publicly discussable topics. When this was combined with the plummeting policy influence of educators and their decreased public status, the balance of power shifted with the result that ministers of education pushed through significant program changes over the loud public protests of members of the teaching profession. Whereas the traditional policy scenario in Canadian education saw the educational professional dominating the process, the recession saw this position changed; the elected provincial politicians now exert the dominant influence. These elected officials respond far more directly to the influence efforts of other constituencies such as the business community and the media rather than to professional educators and local boards of education. Consequently, the policy-making process in most provinces in 1984 reflects strong political, as opposed to professional, dominance.

Recentralization of Decision-Making

Although the vast majority of provincial governments implemented different wage restraint programs and cost control procedures, the impacts of these policies have been similar: increases in provincial control relative to local boards of education, limitations to the bargaining privileges of teachers, and revisions to provincial curricula. The levers permitting these dramatic shifts have been the recession with its deleterious effects on governmental revenues coupled with massive unemployment in the private sector, a decline in the status of public sector employees in large measure due to their militancy during the 1970s and a decline in the respect accorded to teachers and their organizations by the general public. These factors, combined with the perceived public expressed need for drastic action (government leadership or intervention) during a time of national economic crisis brought on by the recession, have resulted in major alterations in the balance of power between the two policy-making bodies primarily responsible, in the legal sense, for the administration of Canadian education — the provinces and local school boards.

The situation described by Lawton (1983), concerning the province of Ontario, is characteristic of the dilemma confronting virtually all Canadian provinces today.

> Increasingly, efficient operation seems to have been bought at the cost of increasing inequities in the funding of education. While there are obvious solutions to this issue, they generally call for the sacrifice of school board fiscal autonomy, an autonomy that is held dear to those who believe that local self government is a right that undergirds the exercise of democratic government at the provincial and federal levels. (p. 39)

The operational reality is more stark than the hypothetical scenario portrayed by Lawton. In a recent national study of trends in Canadian educational finance, Ratsoy (1983, p. 17) concluded, 'These efforts to contain the rising level of cost . . . have resulted in a move toward greater centralization of decision-making in the various provinces and a corresponding decrease in flexibility by local school boards'. The reality of local self-government in education has already been substantially altered. The loss of autonomy is being publicly lamented by elected school board members and local administrators alike. Given the prevailing political climate, their potential to change the altered decision-making relationships is viewed by this writer as being poor in the near future.

Changes in the Relationship Between the Federal and Provincial Governments

The policy-making process has experienced a fourth major impact. This change is reflected in the altered balance between the federal and provincial levels of government — two levels of government which both found themselves in cash starved positions due to the recession. As has been the case in most western democracies, the revenue position of the Canadian federal government deteriorated markedly during the recession. The federal government was forced to implement a wide range of cost-cutting measures. In at least three areas: (a) teacher salaries and working conditions; (b) post-secondary education funding; and (c) interprovincial funding differences, these federal cost reduction measures have had either profound indirect or direct impacts.

(a)   The most dramatic impact on provincial education policy has resulted indirectly from federal efforts to restrain wages in the public sector. In the summer of 1982, the federal government passed Bill C-124, a bill which restricted wage increases and suspended collective bargaining rights for two years in the federal civil service. Because very few teachers (proportionally) are employed by the federal government, it might be predicted that little direct impact would be felt on public education in the provinces. However, the indirect impact was enormous. The federal government, in its budget of 28 June 1982, urged voluntary wage restraint on the private sector. This federal action came following the failure of the federal government during February 1982, at the height of the recession, to persuade the provinces to adopt public sector wage controls.

> Subsequent to the February meeting, however, several provinces, notably British Columbia and Quebec, decided to implement their own public sector wage controls. By the time of the first ministers' meeting of 30 June [1982] most provinces made some moves to restrict public sector compensation. [However] while the premiers were more conciliatory toward the federal government than they had been in February, they would not agree to be bound by the 6 and 5 per cent straitjacket [6 per cent in the first year of the restraint program and 5 per cent in the second year]. (Brown, 1982, p. 17)

The provincially imposed restrictions which were subsequently adopted, reflected the new fiscal and political reality which saw the public service, particularly the previously untouchable teaching profession as being 'fair game'. Eight of the ten provinces limited their grant increases for education to no more than the 6 per cent in the federal guidelines. Several, British Columbia, Alberta, Quebec, Nova Scotia and Newfoundland, imposed even more stringent restraints! The provincial governments, it would seem, recognizing the apparent swing in public sentiment which generally supported the federal government action and being sensitive to the growing public shift in attitudes toward fiscal conservatism, rode the coattails of the federal wage restraint initiatives to implement restraint measures of their own which *directly* impacted upon education. In the process, but partly as a consequence of the federal government 'steering effect', the traditionally strong influence of education lobbies was completely overridden by strong political forces at the provincial level.

Commenting on the apparent change in climate which allowed these dramatic changes to take place, Brown, himself an official of the Canadian Teachers' Federation wrote:

> The federal government and most of the provincial governments know that organized labour will oppose any form of wage controls or limitation on free collective bargaining. They have gambled that with both the law and a large share of public opinion on their side they can weather any conflict with organized labour. They reason that labour's defences have been seriously attacked, possibly weakened, by the state of the economy. Industrial workers seriously hurt by layoffs will have little heart for strike action or other sanctions. In addition, the federal government, in particular, is well aware of the internal divisions among public and private sector employees in the labour movement. Finally, all of the business interests in the country favour public sector wage controls, perhaps a return to mandatory controls on all wages. Government knows it has the support of big business (*ibid*, p. 17)

In retrospect, the gamble paid handsome political returns to provincial governments as well. It allowed some publicly visible savings to be made and it rebuked a group, namely teachers, which many of the public and elected politicians had seen as becoming too powerful for the public good. The point to be emphasized here is that the climate which allowed these provincial actions to take place was assisted by the strong federal government action which resulted in a steering effect at the provincial level.

(b) A second change involving the federal and provincial governments occurred with reference to post-secondary education. At the post-secondary level, the federal government has historically maintained a strong presence. Under the Fiscal Arrangements and Established Programs Financing Act, the federal government has transferred annually to the provinces monies to support post-secondary education and health care. Given the different lengths of high school programs in Canada's ten provincial school systems, several provinces have been able to use some of these federal monies to support part of their secondary school programs. (For example, Ontario has received some monies to support grade 13, the final year of its high school program which is accepted as being equivalent to first year university work.)

Since 1967 in Canada, the federal government has provided approximately 50 per cent of the cost of post-secondary education. (Approximately 3.9 billion dollars for post-secondary education in 1983/84.) While the federal government has allocated the monies for this purpose, the provinces are able to spend these monies as they see fit inasmuch as education is constitutionally a provincial power. This was reinforced by the federal Minister of Finance in the House of Commons when he stated,

> The provinces remain free to allocate funds they receive from the federal government to education, highways, publicity or whatever they want.... It is up to the provinces to decide if they really want to use that money for post-secondary education. Some provinces are doing better than others in this regard. (cited in EPF transfers come under 6 and 5, 1983, p. 15.)

Since 1977, the federal government has contributed an increasingly larger share of the total government support for post-secondary education. At the same time, federal officials have consistently, publicly pointed out that the federal government gets little public (or political) credit for these expenditures. The negotiation of the federal government share of funding for post secondary education has become increasingly rancorous. This came to a head as a result of the recession. Successive federal ministers of finance announced their government's intention to unilaterally reduce annual transfers of funds to the provinces in support of both health and post-secondary education. The federal government in 1983, applied its overall restraint legislation to the education component of federal transfer payments to provinces, capping the growth of per capita payments at 6 per cent in 1983/84 and 5 per cent in 1984/85. This resulted in a net loss in revenue to the provinces estimated to be at approximately $92m. The federal Finance Minister attributed this move directly to the recession. 'Given the size of the current federal budgetary deficit, it was essential to apply the same principles of restraint in this area as we have in others' he stated in Parliament (cited in EPF transfers come under 6 and 5, 1983, p. 15).

These moves have dealt post-secondary education in the ten provinces a severe blow. When linked with the provincial restraint moves noted earlier, there are strong fears that major, long-term damage will be done to the country's universities. Already, the free accessibility notion is under duress with many universities curtailing first year enrolments in order to cope with budget restraint. As in the case of public sector wage restraints, which dramatically affected elementary and secondary education, so at the post-secondary level the federal government has had an indirect but major steering effect by restricting, without a negotiated agreement, the funds it allocates to the provinces for educational purposes. Further, it has created a climate which has encouraged provincial governments to reduce their commitments to post-secondary education (a move urged by some critics for a number of years) while at the same time being able to point the finger of blame at an extra-provincial agency.

Negotiations continue as to what the relationship between the federal government and the ten provincial governments should be in the future on this matter. Current indications suggest that the relationship, already substantially altered, will never return to the pre-recession patterns. Indeed, the federal cabinet still appears to be determined to be much more directive in the post-secondary education activities it supports (such as research), thus exercising a continuing steering effect on what is constitutionally a provincial prerogative. This tendency has been reinforced by a Parliamentary Task Force, established during the recession to review federal-provincial fiscal arrangements. It noted that the federal government has among its interests '... specific roles and responsibilities, not for reflective scholarship, but for mission-oriented enquiry, not for curiosity-oriented research, but for applied research and development, not for general knowledge, but skills in demand in the economy' (Parliamentary Task Force, 1983, p. 123). Indeed, the university community in Canada is beginning to feel the reality that 'he who pays the piper intends to call the tune'. The lever permitting this change to occur was the recession.

Operationally, the federal government has been gradually withdrawing from 'education related' programs since 1977 into more technically oriented programs — ostensibly to assist in the country's economic growth but in reality to put their money into more visible training programs. In August 1982, the federal government passed the National Training Act, 'to better meet the need for skills created by a changing economy and to increase the earning and employment potential of individual workers' (National Training Act, 1982, p. 2). The evolution of this change in federal emphasis is comprehensively described in Rees (1983, chapter 4), who argues that post-secondary education in both the universities and community colleges is being controlled by implicit federal policies.

(c) A third change in the relationship between the federal and provincial government was also precipitated by the recession. This change involved the transfer of revenues to mitigate interregional differences in support for public services caused by differing abilities to pay. As federal revenues dropped, the federal government in 1982 renegotiated the Federal-Provincial Fiscal Arrangements Act. Whereas historically, there had been a trend toward greater equality of spending per pupil in Canada, this gap has now been reopened. This gap is attributable '. . . to the growing inability and unwillingness of the federal government, due to policies of fiscal restraint, to maintain the level of interprovincial revenue equalization at the levels established in the early 1970s'. (Brown, 1983, p. 15). It is predicted that the re-negotiated Act will cause the poorer provinces to become even poorer relative to the richer provinces, most of which are more endowed with natural resources and industrial wealth. Thus, Canadians are experiencing a retreat from what had been previously an accepted national objective: the narrowing of the interregional differences in education which were occasioned by different regional abilities to pay.

This move by the federal government, caused by decreased revenue brought on by the recession, to restrict equalization payments has placed even more fiscal pressure on provincial ministries of education. These federal cutbacks have further curtailed the manoeuvring room of already financially strapped provincial governments.

Conclusion

Canada has experienced recessions and depressions before, as have most western democracies. Has the recession of the 1980s impacted on the education policy-making process? Most assuredly, yes. But the impact must be viewed from two perspectives. First, the fundamental governance structures for education have remained virtually unchanged. What has changed are the relative influence positions of each of the three levels of government — federal, provincial and local and the influence of the various players in the policy-making process.

While the federal government has little formal presence in educational matters, it has exerted tremendous leverage on educational matters during the recession through its power to control certain cash flows and its ability to enact pieces of legislation which altered public opinion. The federal government, through its restraint actions, established a climate which allowed dramatic changes to occur in the status of public sector employees such as teachers. Further, through its actions in renegotiating agreements with the provinces, the federal government has increased the revenue dilemma of the provinces even more than might have occurred if those jurisdictions were dealing with recessionary pressures under traditional funding patterns. Provincial governments have been forced by the federal government into more draconian stances than they might otherwise have taken on issues of wage control, bargaining rights, interprovincial spending differences and spending per pupil within a given province. Thus, it can be concluded that the steering effect of the federal government, even though it has little direct constitutional authority on educational matters, has allowed it to wield substantially *more* influence on educational policy than previously.

All of these factors forced provincial governments to invoke long-standing constitutional powers which, since the British North America Act of 1867, have given provincial governments majority control of educational matters. Historically, a negotiated accommodation had developed which saw local boards exercising a high degree of local control, particularly over financial matters. As has been noted elsewhere, Canadian provincial legislatures have been characterized as being benevolently omnipotent on educational matters. With the recession, the fragility of this benevolence has been dramatically illustrated with local autonomy being severely eroded. There appears to be incontrovertible evidence that even though the recession has not wrought any fundamental structural changes to the education policy-making process, it has significantly altered the way in which those processes operated in the last decade to patterns more reminiscent of the days before 1960 when a high degree of provincial control existed. There seems to be a consensus of all interests that local autonomy has been an obvious casualty of the recession.

If the education policy-making structures have remained intact, relative influence positions have shifted significantly. Who have been the winners and losers in Canadian education? Clearly, provincial governments have recentralized operationally their constitutional omnipotence. This recentralization (vis-à-vis the 1970s) has been at the direct expense of local boards. But local authorities have not been the only losers — their considerable influence prior to the recession was only by gentlemen's agreement and precedent.

Nationally, it would appear to this writer, that teachers as local or provincial influence groups have lost immensely. Where they previously had exercised major influence on curriculum matters and job related questions, now, elected politicians are enacting changes despite teacher protests and arguments. Further, the heretofore 'sacred' status of teachers in terms of job security, negotiation rights and salary levels has been dealt a devastating blow. This has been complemented by an apparent shift in public opinion which has redefined the teaching position as no longer being buffered from the financial pressures facing society at large. It will take a long time for teachers to regain the lost ground, even if a financial recovery is imminent.

Even within the provincial civil services, the influence of educators has waned. Elected officials, the ministers of education and their cabinet colleagues are directing the educational policy-making process on a scale not seen in Canadian education for decades. Elected provincial figures are now very much in control of educational policy. While constitutionally this has always been the case, operationally, as is the case in most parliamentary democracies, the civil service had exercised a dominant steering effect on educational policy. As a result of the recession, education became visibly vulnerable as a cost centre. Further, political gain and financial savings were to be made by 'educator bashing'. This has seen a rise in the operational influence of ministers of education, and a concomitant decrease in that of the education professionals, particularly educational civil servants. As ministers have moved to exert more of their own authority while discounting the influence of members of the public education community, they have accorded increased influence to other groups such as the business community.

A final significant change which the recession has wrought to the education policy-making process in Canada is the altered role of the federal government. The recession saw the Ottawa government move unilaterally to play a stronger steering role on educational matters than previously — witness the federal government's role in wage restraint, post-secondary education finance and in the equalization of expenditures for education among the ten provinces. In so doing, the federal government has exercised considerable indirect influence on Canadian education, for apparently politically acceptable arguments. At the same time, it has managed to transfer to the provinces most of the political heat generated by the education cutbacks. (Ironically, the same phenomenon has occurred in the relationship between provincial governments and local school authorities. The provinces have centralized authority and power while the local boards have taken increased public criticism!) Thus, the federal government appears to have been a 'winner' all around. It has cut expenditures, used its influence to create opinion climates in support of restraint which caused provincial governments to act in ways they had been unwilling to previously and, in the process, the federal government has managed to avoid public blame in all areas except post-secondary education.

In summary, Canada's policy-making structures have changed little in the recession. However, their operation and the roles and influence exercised by the various players in educational policy formulation have changed significantly. Canada has moved from a tradition of professional dominance of most educational policies to one now of overt elected politician dominance represented by swings to the right in fiscal policies, curricular policies and on many personnel matters. While these policy-making changes are occurring, the nation staggers to recover from the recession. Productivity increases lag, unemployment remains in excess of 10 per cent, teacher morale continues to plummet, public scepticism over the quality of education grows and youth unemployment remains at unprecedently high levels. In Canadian education, even though the recession has wrought some major changes in balance to the policy-making processes and to the products of those processes, the recession's most lasting impact may well be to foreshadow a national concern for the quality and mission of public school systems in a manner similar to that which is occurring south of the forty-ninth parallel.

Thomas R. Williams

Acknowledgements

The writer acknowledges the helpful comments provided on earlier drafts of this paper from colleagues Bill Peruniak, Ruth Rees, Brian Sharples, Richard Townsend and Leroy Whitehead.

References

BROWN, W. (1982) *Teachers and the Deterioration of the Canadian Economy: Is There a Better Way?* unpublished manuscript, Ottawa, Canadian Teachers Federation.

BROWN, W.J. (1983) 'The educational toll of the "Great Recession"', in *The Cost of Controlling the Costs of Education in Canada*, Toronto, Ontario Institute For Studies in Education, pp. 1–22.

CARRIGAN, E. (1983) 'Canada's spending on education must be trimmed', *Kitchener Waterloo Record*, August.

EPF transfers come under 6 and 5. (1983) *University Affairs*, May, p. 15.

GOLDFARB, M. (1984) 'Public school system has failed to train youth for a job, Canadians say', *Toronto Star*, 18 May.

GOVERNMENT OF CANADA (1982) *National Training Act, An Act to Establish a National Program for Occupational Training*, Ottawa, 22 June.

HARRIS, C. (1983) 'Where industries are headed', *The Financial Post: Report On The Nation*, winter 1983/84, p. 32.

LAWTON, S. (1983) 'Ontario's approach: Paying school boards to Save', in *The Cost of Controlling the Costs of Education in Canada*, Toronto, Ontario Institute for Studies in Education, pp. 33–45.

LUCAS, B. (1977). 'The confederation: Ottawa and the provinces', *Politics of Education Bulletin*, 7, 2, pp. 12–16.

MICHAUD, P. (1983). 'Educational finance in Quebec and New Brunswick: Similarities and differences', in, *The Cost of Controlling the Costs of Education in Canada*, Toronto, Ontario Institute for Studies in Education, pp. 49–63.

ONTARIO (1984) *Economic Transformation: Technological Innovation and Diffusion in Ontario.* Toronto, Ministry of Treasury and Economics.

ORGANIZATION FOR ECONOMIC COOPERATION AND DEVELOPMENT (1975), *OECD External Examiners' Report on Educational Policy in Canada*, Toronto, Canadian Association for Adult Education.

ORGANIZATION FOR ECONOMIC COOPERATION AND DEVELOPMENT (1983) 'International perspectives', *OECD Observer*, March, p. 28.

PARLIAMENTARY TASK FORCE ON FEDERAL-PROVINCIAL FISCAL ARRANGEMENTS (1981), *Report*, Ottawa, Queen's Printer.

RATSOY, E. (1983). 'Recent trends in financing Canadian education', *Canadian School Executive*, 3, 5, pp. 17–18.

REES, R. (1983), *The Interorganizational Collectivity: A Study of the Manpower Institutional Training System in Manitoba*, unpublished doctoral disseration, University of Toronto.

WILLIAMS, T.R., (1977) 'The local districts: Gaining in public visibility', *Politics of Education Bulletin*, 7, 2, pp. 2–5.

3 Hong Kong: The Political Economy of Education

Ming Chan
University of Hong Kong

Michael Kirst
Stanford University, USA

Background

Hong Kong, with its population of 5½ million (98 per cent of them Chinese) in an area of 400 square miles (about the same as New York city), seems to have more than its share of social and economic problems.[1] As a colony under the British Crown, Hong Kong is composed of three parts that were acquired by the British in three stages: (i) Hong Kong Island (thirty-two square miles) from the 1842 Treaty of Nanking which ended the Opium War and started the humiliating century of 'Unequal Treaties' for China; (ii) Kowloon Peninsula (three and three-quarter square miles across the harbor from the island) from the First Convention of Peking in 1860; and (iii) the New Territories (365 square miles, covering the land area north of Kowloon and over 200 adjacent islands) from a ninety-nine year lease under the Second Convention of Peking in 1898. Legally, most of the present British-administered territory of Hong Kong must revert to China on 1 July 1997, when the leasehold expires, while in theory, the Hong Kong Island and the Kowloon Peninsula are ceded to the British in perpetuity. However, with the international airport, the container terminus, the main water supply reservoirs, the majority of industrial concerns and population located in the soon-to-expire leased territory, the island and peninsula part of Hong Kong can hardly function in isolation. Thus, the 1997 issue transcends legal necessities and assumes crisis proportion. There is a lack of confidence in the future of Hong Kong as an international market economy and open free society under Chinese Communist rule. This has led to widespread panic and depression among the local Chinese population. This uncertainty over the '1997 China Syndrome' could not have come at a worse moment, because Hong Kong is still suffering from the most severe economic recession in recent history.

To many people, the business of Hong Kong has been from the very beginning — business. The original British purpose in the acquisition of Hong Kong was to facilitate the China trade with its strategically located deep-water harbor. Indeed, during the first century of British rule, Hong Kong grew from barren rocks, prospered on China trade, and gradually emerged as the preeminent international port and economic center of the South China Coast. With the British presence came Western-style commercial and financial institutions, public utilities and modern transportation facilities which together laid the foundation of Hong Kong's success as an entrepot. The British colonial government in Hong Kong, headed by a British governor appointed by London and with its upper echelon staffed by British expatriates, provided a fairly efficient and stable administration. But it was and still is *not* democratic — without any popularly elected representation of the local Chinese in key decision-making processes. The relative peace, stability and prosperity of Hong Kong, even when the Chinese mainland was in turmoil during foreign wars and revolutions, attracted a massive influx of capital and immigrants from the neighboring Kwangtong province.

In a sense, Hong Kong seems to have prospered through the misfortunes of China. Following the outbreak of the Sino-Japanese War in 1937, and the colony's occupation under the Japanese in 1941, Hong Kong enjoyed a period of unprecedented prosperity as the only free port on the China coast, while its population almost doubled to 1.6m in 1941, with a massive influx of refugees from war-torn China. The Kuomintang-Chinese Communist Civil War and the 1949 Communist takeover of the mainland saw another exodus into Hong Kong. This emigré Chinese manpower, capital, and entrepreneurial skills provided the backbone of Hong Kong's spectacular growth and development in the past three decades. The United Nations' embargo against the People's Republic of China during the Korean War drastically curtailed Hong Kong's external trade and nearly ended its entrepot role. With typical resiliency, Hong Kong turned immediately to new industries with emphasis on consumer products and textiles. Since then, a remarkably successful transformation from a port of trade to a center of light export industries has underlined

Hong Kong's almost uninterrupted economic growth. The export of local industrial products, transportation services, tourism, and, since the last decade, international financial services provide the substance of employment opportunities for the fast growing population, which enjoys one of the highest GNP per capita in Asia.

This strong economy, presided over by an adaptable colonial bureaucracy, and reinforced by the traditional Chinese family system, has enabled Hong Kong to weather several storms — the 1965/66 banking crisis, the 1967 leftist riots (inspired by the Cultural Revolution on the Chinese mainland), the 1973 stock market crash and the worldwide energy crisis. Yet, the strains and stresses of the past three decades of imbalanced growth and unplanned development, long hidden behind the facade of prosperity, are beginning to surface while the demographic fabrics of Hong Kong are undergoing new changes. The absorption of the recent 1977/81 waves of 'illegal immigrants' (many of them poorly educated and ill-suited for Hong Kong's urban capitalism), and the accommodation of the needs of a baby-boom, local-born generation placed very heavy burdens on limited public resources.[2] Indeed, their sheer size (often with vocal and militant claims) has seriously distorted the already overloaded social services, housing, education and community facilities.

These multiple forces came precisely at the collapse of the local real estate market which had been the major engine of the 1978/81 prosperity. The government's land policy propelled a property market boom that in turn buoyed the stock market and the construction trade.[3] But overspeculation from overpriced and overbuilt units reached its zenith and burst in late 1981, dragging down the construction trade, stock market, and government revenues. Unfortunately, 1981/82 was also the rock bottom of the US economic recession that had negative worldwide effects, leading to very substantial decreases in Hong Kong's exports. Unemployment and underemployment among manufacturing and service workers became a serious problem, and the government had to operate with an unaccustomed massive deficit.[4] The Hong Kong dollar skidded down 20 per cent in its international exchange rate. It is against such a retrenched economy, coupled with a somewhat troubled social scene, that the 1997 crisis of confidence concerning China broke out in 1982. At the same time a panel of overseas reviewers called for a major overhaul and increase in resources for the education system.

Table 3.1: Student Flow Statistics (Drawn from Education Department Sources)

1 Actual and estimated retention rates of grade cohort for both sexes from Primary 1 to Form 7 in public and private schools, Hong Kong, 1965 to 1981

| School year pupils entered P.1 | Retention per 1000 pupils who entered Primary 1 | | | | | | | | | | | | | F.3 (Year attending F.3) | F.4 | Possible Outlet for Form 3 Leavers | | | |
| | | | | | | | | | | | | | | | | Technical Institute | | | Total |
	P.1	P.2	P.3	P.4	P.5	P.6	F.1	F.2	F.3	F.4	F.5	F.6	F.7			Full Time (Enrolment)	Part Time Day (Provision)	Part Time Evening (Enrolment)	
1965	1000	805	812	788	729	645	494	423	364	319	293	95	39	364(73)	319	3	4	23	349
1967	1000	854	862	838	798	724	559	494	450	394	382	125	47	450(75)	394	5	4	24	427
1969	1000	892	905	892	859	795	627	580	546	500	470	139	61	546(77)	500	7	19	30	556
1971	1000	927	945	948	936	861	789	755	711	622	605	197	89	711(79)	622	9	28	35	694
1973	1000	951	958	954	918	873	916	850	771	692	685	223	103	771(81)	692	11	59	49	811
1975	1000	951	963	970	946	909	964	929	848	760	753	245	115	848(83)	760	14	73	58	905
1977	1000	974	1006	1017	984	949	1009	975	889	819	811	264	124	889(85)	819	20	102	63	1004
1979	1000	1001	1013	1013	980	949	1012	979	896	838	832	270	128	896(87)	838	20	100	61	1019
1981	1000	989	998	999	968	940	1004	974	894	852	849	276	132	894(89)	852	20	100	62	1034

2 Actual retention rates of grade and age cohort for both sexes from Primary 1 to Form 4 in public and private schools, Hong Kong, 1971 to 1979

Retention per 1000 pupils who entered Primary 1

Children aged 6 entering P.1 in school year	P.1	P.2	P.3	P.4	P.5	P.6	F.1	F.2	F.3	F.4
1971	1000	826	770	720	697	634	597	564	509	425
1973	1000	858	805	769	724	704	707	651		
1975	1000	872	825	792	747	720				
1977	1000	900	863	826						
1979	1000	919								

3 *Actual retention rates of grade and age cohort for Male from Primary 1 to Form 4 in public and private schools, Hong Kong, 1971 to 1979*

Retention per 1000 pupils who entered Primary 1

Children aged 6 entering P.1 in school year	P.1	P.2	P.3	P.4	P.5	P.6	F.1	F.2	F.3	F.4
1971	1000	814	746	684	659	593	565	512	455	365
1973	1000	846	789	737	684	660	665	595		
1975	1000	864	808	765	713	684				
1977	1000	892	848	799						
1979	1000	908								

4 *Actual retention rates of grade and age cohort for Female from Primary 1 to Form 4 in public and private schools, Hong Kong, 1971 to 1979*

Retention per 1000 pupils who entered Primary 1

Children aged 6 entering P.1 in school year	P.1	P.2	P.3	P.4	P.5	P.6	F.1	F.2	F.3	F.4
1971	1000	840	796	760	738	679	631	621	568	491
1973	1000	871	824	803	768	752	752	712		
1975	1000	880	844	820	783	759				
1977	1000	909	880	855						
1979	1000	932								

Hong Kong's Education System: Rapid Expansion and Unfulfilled Demand

Hong Kong's education structure is based on the conventions of the British colonial administration with several modifications to fit the unique Hong Kong situation. By the end of the Japanese occupation in 1945, the school population had dropped from 120,000 to 4000. The 1949 takeover of mainland China by the Communists caused a huge influx of refugees from the People's Republic, and the total population increased by 50 per cent during the 1950s to three million. By 1963 the school population had reached 800,000, and in the early 1970s, primary education for the 6–11 age group was free and compulsory. The rapidly growing Hong Kong economy permitted government authorities to respond partially to the Chinese population's insistence for more educational opportunity. Table 3.1 displays the growth in school places and retention rates from 1965/1981. Class sizes are in the 40–45 pupil range. An unusual feature is the low percentage (4 per cent) of schools operated directly by the government. Most schools are fully funded by the government but operated privately through religious or other nonprofit boards.

Kindergarten is provided by private entrepreneurs and now enrols 85 per cent of the 4–5 age cohort. Public funding is universal for the primary grades, but note that in table 3.1 only 27 per cent are enrolled in Form VI, or the US 12th grade equivalent. The structure and content of secondary education is considerably affected by the lack of provision and fierce competition for university places. Only 2 per cent of the relevant age group secure a place in Hong Kong's two universities. Indeed, university enrolment could be doubled without a significant drop in the quality of students. The number of qualified applicants at the single polytechnic school is an even higher multiple of the available spaces. The problems mentioned above, however, should *not* obscure the enormous growth in higher education enrolment funded between 1945/1982.

In 1981, the government appointed a panel of four overseas experts to do an overall review of the system (now called the Llewellyn Report after its chairman).[5] This panel began its deliberations right before the 1982 recession. The Llewellyn panel concluded that 'there is an overwhelming case for the expansion of opportunity for study at the higher degree level'. The public pressure for this has been growing more intense since 1982.

While education opportunity is most constricted at the post-secondary level, there are major problems of quantity and quality at the secondary level as well. Because of a lack of facilities and teachers, the government has been forced to 'purchase' places in low quality private schools for some pupils aged 13–16. Pupils are sifted through four exams at different points of their schooling, and the lowest scoring students are directed to 'bought' places in private schools that receive a lower subsidy rate (about one-third of the government schools). Compulsory schooling in Hong Kong now extends through age 14. The Llewellyn panel concluded:

> To have such gross differences among schools providing compulsory education cannot be justified any more than the practice of assigning about half the pupils in compulsory education to schools that do not match the parents' preferences.

In sum, demand for high quality education outstrips supply of places for students beyond Form III or 9th grade (see table 3.2 on actual and projected tertiary enrolment). This has created political pressure for more government education spending just as Hong Kong entered the worldwide recession. This pent-up education demand grew despite the rapid increase in government expenditures presented in table 3.3. Note the recurrent expenditure for education from 1966/1982 increases in real dollars, and as a percentage of the gross national product.

Despite ths impressive progress the Llewellyn panel emphasized that:

> ... the aggregate of resources going into the education system (private and public) is, on a per capita basis, still unimpressive. This is so in terms of criteria such as financial outlays per student, capacity-to-pay of the economy, and sectoral emphases.... On the evidence that we received we formed the conclusion that more could be allocated without detracting from other human-welfare services. The emphases ... should be tilted more favorably towards the junior (rather than senior) and the vocational (rather than the academic) branches of education (IV.11).

The overseas panel's statement of resource availability, however, needs to be reasessed in light of the unfavorable economic events since 1982.

Table 3.2: Actual and Projected Build Up of First Year Places on Courses of Tertiary Education (Full Time & Part Time) 1975/1993

Year	1975		1978		1981		1984		1987		1990		1993	
	Enrol.	Percentage of age group	Enrol.	Percentage of age group	No. of places	Percentage of age group	No. of places	Percentage of age group	No. of places	Percentage of age group	No. of places	Percentage of age group	No. of places	Percentage of age group
1 Post-Form V courses in technical institutes	2714	2.7	4768	4.3	8900	7.5	14260	14.6	15020	18.0	15020	18.1	15020	18.3
2 Polytechnic	n.a.	—	16353	14.7	13040	10.9	13610	14.0	15310	18.3	17220	20.7	19370	23.6
3 Colleges of Education (including Technical Teachers College)	576	0.6	518	0.5	989	0.8	870	0.9	1010	1.2	1010	1.2	1010	1.2
4 School of Nursing	n.a.	—	959	0.9	1400	1.2	2000	2.1	2500	3.0	2500	3.0	2500	3.0
5 Assisted Approved Post-Secondary Colleges	1740	1.7	2386	2.1	2105	1.8	1900	2.0	1900	2.3	1900	2.3	1900	2.3
6 Universities	2132	2.1	2555	2.3	2630	2.2	2910	3.0	3280	3.9	3690	4.4	4150	5.1
TOTAL	7162	7.0	27539	24.7	29064	24.4	35550	36.5	39020	46.7	41340	49.7	43950	53.5

Table 3.3: Government Expenditure on Education

		Capital Expenditure				Recurrent Expenditure			
		Total ($m)	(Percentage GDP)	$ per head of population	$ per student in sector	Total ($m)	(Percentage GDP)	$ per head of population	$ per student in sector
1966/67	School and College	45.413		13	52	889.004		245	1,026
	University	16.531		5	3,885	129.458		36	30,425
	Total	61.944	0.15	17	71	1,018.462	2.24	281	1,170
1971/72	School and College	74.286		18	65	1,319.574		326	1,158
	University	214.737		53	36,941	260.683		64	44,845
	Total	289.023	0.44	71	252	1,580.257	2.24	391	1,380
1976/77	School and College	140.754		32	120	1,967.245		443	1,679
	University and Polytechnic	89.850		20	5,564	528.128		119	32,703
	Total	230.604	0.22	60	194	2,495.373	2.54	562	2,101
1981/82	School and College	375.510		73	307	2,800.455		546	2,292
	University and Polytechnic	173.847		34	7,946	823.441		160	37,638
	Total	549.357	0.41	107	442	3,623.896	2.68	706	2,914

Note: All dollars shown are 1981/82 constant H.K. dollars.

The Hong Kong Polytechnic began operation in August 1972. Its lower unit cost per student accounts for the drastic drop in the recurrent expenditure per student in the higher education sector in 1976/77 as against 1971/72.

57

Impact of Worldwide Economic Recession

Our major theme is that Hong Kong rode through the recession without unfavorable economic impacts large enough to forestall education improvement, but the pressure for education reform has been delayed by the economic uncertainty caused by the '1997 China phobia'. There is an interaction effect, however, between these two economic phenomena. In August 1982, the *Far Eastern Economic Review* expressed it this way:

> The collapse of the Hong Kong stockmarket — with the Hang Seng Index down 95 points on 9 and 10 August for a 180-point fall over the past two weeks — has not been primarily political. But it has shown how political factors exaggerate underlying trends. Just as two years ago any vague noises out of China that investors could put their hearts at ease added fuel to a raging property-based bull market, now any noises about possible changes in Hong Kong's status are grist to the bears.
>
> The psychology is simple enough: while money can be made faster in Hong Kong than almost anywhere else, investors can afford to discount the political risk. But once profits fade, confidence soon follows. 1977 is one problem; world recession, high interest rates and a weak Street are others.
>
> All told, the property merry-go-round is moving into reverse, with those who bought at the top hurting from interest costs and those relying on trading earnings hurting from lack of sales. (13 August 1982)

In a 1982 poll, the *Far Eastern Economic Review* reported (13 March 1982) that only 2 per cent of Hong Kong residents said it was best for Hong Kong to be returned to China when the lease runs out, but 66 per cent desired no change in Hong Kong's status. Obviously, this public concern about a takeover by the People's Republic of China will have enduring and deep effects on Hong Kong's economic growth.

The 1982 recession dramatically slowed a rapidly growing Hong Kong economy, but did not throw it into reverse. Domestic exports declined 3 per cent in real terms for 1982, the first decline since 1975. Manufacturing employment fell 5 per cent in 1982, but this was mostly offset by an increase in service employment. Inflation fell from 15 per cent in 1981 to 9 per cent in late 1982.[6] Overall, the 1982

Hong Kong economy grew at a 2.4 per cent real growth rate! However, the government commented:

> This represents a very significant slowing down compared with the double digit growth rates recorded successively for each year since 1976. (1982 *Economic Background*, p. 5)

Total exports declined by 2 per cent in real terms, compared with an increase of 13 per cent in 1981. Unemployment rose from 3.5 per cent to 4 per cent, but the government noted that there was an increase in 'underemployment'. The most drastic recessionary impacts were felt in declining property and stock values.[7]

Overall, the recession's impact was not sufficient to cause a drastic rethinking of education policy as evidenced in some other countries. Since the unsettled 1997 negotiations led to a 'loss of investor nerve', government revenues were hit especially hard because of heavy government reliance on the sale of property to finance recurrent expenditures.[8] The government could not sell much publicly owned land in 1981/84. Primary education operating budgets for 1983/84 will increase only by 3.3 per cent. Total education expenditures were proposed by the government to increase Hong Kong $5.161 billion in 1982/83 to $5.552 billion in 1983/84. The growing deficit, however, may hinder the government's ability to meet even this modest increase.

Compared to some of the recession-impacted states in the United States, this 1983/84 increase in education funds is quite high. From 1981/83, US state/local education expenditures dropped in real terms. Hong Kong's problem is how to meet rising expectations for education with a slower growth economy caused by 1997 political concerns and world economic conditions.[9]

The Overseas Panel's Education Recommendations

Part of the rising public expectation was fuelled by the overseas panel headed by Sir John Llewellyn of the United Kingdom. The panel's 139 page report included numerous recommendations such as:

1   The language of the heart (i.e. mother tongue) should be used in all schools as the medium of instruction throughout the entire period of compulsory schooling (i.e. Primary 1 to Form 3). Also from Form 1 to Form 3, there should be a

gradual shift to genuine bilingual programs so that by the end of Form 3 the students are receiving about half of their instruction in Chinese and half in English.

2 Senior secondary places (grades 10–12) should be increased to allow all students to complete secondary education, if they so wish. Steps must be taken to ameliorate the pressure of numerous examinations.

3 The scheme for 'bought places' in secondary schools should be improved. All junior secondary places should be given the same amount of resources, so as to raise the standards of some private independent schools.

4 Reasonable salary scales should be formulated for kindergarten teachers and childcare workers to improve the compensation package for these personnel. Training facilities for pre-school teachers should be strengthened, and public subsidy extended, by steps, to include kindergarten education.

5 Opportunities for tertiary education should be expanded. The inauguration of the second polytechnic (City Polytechnic of Hong Kong) should be expedited, and a third university planned immediately. Public support should be given to approved post-secondary institutions to raise their social and academic status to degree-awarding level.

6 Continuing education services should be expanded and diversified. An Open University should be established and external degrees implemented, so as to increase access to 'second chance' education.

7 The quality of pre-service teacher training should be improved and degrees in education introduced at colleges of education. In-service training for teachers should be strengthened so as to enhance the status of teachers and the prestige of the teaching profession.

8 Research and survey activities should be encouraged and strengthened. Goals and objectives of the education system should be formulated, and long range plans developed.

Many of these recommendations would be quite costly. They were not, however, stimulated or affected by the recession. The overseas panel studied Hong Kong during the 1981 economic growth period when government monetary resource constraints appeared minimal. If the Llewellyn panel's views are crucial in rethinking Hong Kong's education policy, then the recession will not be a prime factor in new policies. The panel's criticisms of the education system in Hong Kong were made in the context of a dynamic and growing economy, and the panel was very impressed with the enterprise, flexibility, and growth in Hong Kong's economy.[10]

As of late 1983, Hong Kong's government has not blamed their belated response to the panel's report on the recession. The government stressed the need to have extensive public reactions to the panel's comprehensive recommendations. The Llewellyn report sparked the longest debate in Hong Kong's Legislative Council history. At the debate's conclusion, the government accepted a resolution that the report should be the basis for future education policy in Hong Kong.

In short, a report written before the recession negatively impacted Hong Kong is the major substantive basis for reconsidering Hong Kong's education policy. Public responses have been unusually large and tense as far as any Hong Kong Government proposal goes. Over 400 written comments and critiques were submitted, and several dozen public meetings/seminars/press conferences were held by various social and educational groups to air their views on the report.

The general verdict is very positive, in part, because the public felt that the panel had endorsed their legitimate claims. Many of these complaints and proposals had been ignored or not implemented by the Hong Kong government. Public testimony demonstrates that Hong Kong residents want a strong and positive government response in such areas as: (i) language of teaching through Form III be Chinese; (ii) fewer exams; (iii) free schooling through Form V or even VI and VII; and (iv) a third university.

So far the Hong Kong government has not *yet* used 1997 as a *public* excuse to delay or postpone any educational undertaking that it initiated. Indeed, the second polytechnic opened in August/ September 1984 in rented premises while a new campus has been under construction in Kowloon. The talk in official circles about the third university seems to be gaining momentum, but there is no clear signal yet on a campus site.

In response to strong and growing public pressure and as a gesture of official concern, the government in spring 1984 set up a high-powered fourteen-member Commission to coordinate and advise on overall education policy in reference to the Llewellyn Report. This Commission has six months to: (i) define overall educational objectives, formulate education policy and recommend priorities for implementation with regard to available resources; (ii) to coordinate and monitor the planning and development of education at all levels; and (iii) to initiate educational research. As considerable time has lapsed since the Llewellyn report was first submitted in November 1982, the Hong Kong public at large will be seriously disappointed if the government does not take positive actions since the task of this Commission was completed by October 1984.

Economic Uncertainty and 1997

While the general lack of confidence in the future of Hong Kong after 1997 still depresses the public mood, realists no longer debate the inevitability of future China assumption of sovereignty over Hong Kong. To many, the core issue at stake is how to get from here to 1997, and a realistic formula is yet to be found that will permit the Chinese national flag to fly over Hong Kong while private business continues to thrive. So far, despite (i) the joint Sino-British vow of maintaining the 'stability and prosperity' of Hong Kong; (ii) official Chinese pronouncements that 'Hong Kong people will rule Hong Kong'; and (iii) other verbal PRC assurances that the present lifestyle of the Hong Kong people will remain unchanged after 1997, the public has responded with deep scepticism.

On 26 September 1984 China and the United Kingdom signed a formal treaty ending British rule. In exchange, China has promised that Hong Kong may maintain its capitalist economic system, its status as a free port, its separate currency, its legal system and many of its civil liberties for fifty years after 1997. Hong Kong will become what will be called a special administrative region within China. But there is no way that Britain can enforce this treaty if China decides to undermine the capitalist economy.

As of early 1984, the property market continues to be depressed, and the Hong Kong dollar continues to slide (to an all-time record low of 9.6 to one US dollar).[11] New investments from both local and international sources virtually stopped, and outflow of both capital and professional talent overseas increased drastically during the past two years.[12] The net result of all these negative economic bearings on government revenues and expenditures is obvious. Hong Kong is renowned for low taxes, but since the government owned considerable land, it could sell land to finance public expenditures at a reasonable level. The ability of the government to sell land at high prices that generated a major portion of public income for financing much of the government's capital investment during the late 1970s has been stopped. The record budget deficit of HK$4 billion requires the government to cut back on major undertakings. Many projects have to be postponed or even cancelled, and a freeze on hiring has been instituted in many government departments.

If the stereotype image of Hong Kong as a 'laissez-faire' paradise were still valid, then there would be much less cause for concern. However, the Hong Kong Government, in order to cope with changed circumstances and new demands, has quietly but effectively departed from 'laissez-faire'.[13] It has adopted an increasingly active and 'positive interventionist' approach to many areas of public affairs and economic life since the early 1970s. While taxation and government regulation are comparatively lighter than in many other countires, public sector expenditures accounted for almost a quarter (24.2 per cent) of Hong Kong's GDP for 1982, roughly the same share of GDP as in South Korea, Singapore, Taiwan — the other three (and decidedly 'non laissez-faire') members of the so-called 'gang of four' of newly and rapidly industrializing economies of Asia.[14] The Hong Kong government's land policy during the 1977/81 period more than just interfered, but directly controlled and shaped the real estate boom which fuelled a double-digit inflation. This policy led to runaway rents that required the government to impose extensive rent control measures.[15] Furthermore, more than 40 per cent of the population is accommodated in public housing, and a number of new towns and the new Mass Transit Railway Subway System were all completely built by the government. One may suspect that the Hong Kong Government did not openly discard the myth of 'laissez-faire' for two reasons: it could be useful in attracting overseas investments, and the government wants to avoid the rising expectations of the public, which would demand more from an acknowledged 'interventionist' administration.

As the uncertainty over the 1997 China Syndrome becomes stronger, the Hong Kong government may have no other choice in the remaining years before 1997 than to assume an even more decisive and active 'interventionist' approach. Such an approach might help to arrest the decline of public confidence and economic performance. The very recent government takeover of the ailing Hang Long Bank and the pegging of the Hong Kong dollar at 7.80 to the US dollar are clear indications along this line.

If the official vow of maintaining the 'stability and prosperity' of Hong Kong before the changes in 1997 has any bearing on public policy, then housing and education must remain top priority items on the government agenda. The social calm and stability of the past three decades has been the result of both the traditional Chinese family system as well as the upward socioeconomic mobility and employment opportunities provided by a growing economy. The continued requirements of upward mobility, the technological upgrading in the manufacturing sector, and the increased complexity of the service sector all create heavy demands for better educated workers. This can only be provided with an expanded and refined educational system with accountability to the public at large. In view of the depressed public mood over the 1997 issues, and the increasingly inadequate stabilizing influence of the Chinese family system under the onslaught of the more Westernized local-born generation now coming of age, a strong and vibrant economy — providing opportunities for employment and upward mobility — will be a major force in preserving Hong Kong's free and open society until 1997. In this sense, educational reforms are closely linked with the future of Hong Kong, and the fate of five million people who will not and cannot migrate to escape the China Syndrome.

The Future of Education Policy in Hong Kong

From a purely economic perspective, the local economy has been on the rebound since the last months of 1983, with exports registering a substantial increase, the pegged HK dollars remaining stable, and a top level official even forecasting a modest boom for 1985/86.[16] But the long-term economic prospect is not encouraging as the same officials worry about dwindling government reserve funds, and the inevitable deficit spending in the last years before 1997. Still, one can believe that the Hong Kong government would prefer an honorable exit while leaving Hong Kong in a stable and healthy socioeconomic condition. If the current Sino-British negotiations on the 1997 issues can lead to mutually acceptable solutions, then the Hong Kong government must move fast to prepare the local people to meet massive change. In this longer term scenario, educational reform both as a process in itself, and in its expected results, becomes an integral part of the 1997 'stability and prosperity' survival kit.

In a more immediate frame of reference, the *realpolitik* game of winning favorable public opinion vis-à-vis the People's Republic of China at this crucial hour of Sino-British negotiations dictates a strong government initiative for reforming the educational system. As public concern about 1997 becomes more acute, the Hong Kong government's freedom of action may become more constrained in a balancing act between diminishing resources and increasing public demands for programs and involvement. The field of education should become more a product of popular demand and public control which, in a sense, will not be alien to the government's current eleventh hour effort to promote localization and devolution of the administrative machinery. The timely implementation of many of the overseas panel's recommendations to improve the current education scene, such as mother-tongue teaching, will go a long way toward localization, democratization, and making the Hong Kong government more responsive to both local Hong Kong Chinese sentiments and the sensitivity of the PRC. Thus, the rather costly programs of educational reform can be justified by their immediate psycho-political yields as well as the longer term dividends of social stability and economic growth. If, on the other hand, the Hong Kong government becomes passive and merely responds to external forces, it would not only forfeit its last chance to contribute creatively to the future of Hong Kong, but even lose its legitimate claim to be an efficient, enlightened and responsive administration of a free and open society confronting Communist domination. The options open to the Hong Kong government are indeed very limited, for it must act soon and fast along the lines prescribed by popular demands, while its administrative capacity still remains effective.

In sum, education reform should proceed despite the economic and political uncertainty surrounding 1997. The serious weaknesses in the current education system, highlighted by the overseas panel, have been verified by several months of public testimony and from numerous individuals. No matter what form of government ensues in 1997, Hong Kong will need to meet the economic competition from Taiwan, Korea, Singapore and ASEAN nations. These nations will compete in large part through an educated workforce that can change skills quickly to meet the rapidly shifting world trade patterns. Hong Kong's education system must be capable of competing through an educated workforce or as economists term it, 'human capital'.

Moreover, social stability and public support for the colonial regime requires employment and job mobility opportunities that can be provided, in part, by a strengthened education system. An improved education system may require some reallocation of public spending priorities. In the last decade, the government has expanded housing and transportation expenditures at a faster rate than education.[17] A crucial decision will be facing the government on whether to reverse these past public priorities and favor education. Even before such decisions are made on government priorities, however, there are numerous no cost changes that can be made based on the overseas panel's report. For example, a reduction in the number of exams would save money rather than spend it.

No matter what paths these educational reforms will eventually take, one fundamental and urgent point shall remain clear — the present education system in Hong Kong has to be overhauled both quantitatively and qualitatively, and this must be done wholeheartedly and done very soon.

Notes

1 For an economic history of Hong Kong, see HOPKINS K. (Ed.), (1971) *Hong Kong: An Industrial Colony*, Hong Kong, Oxford University Press, 1971.

2 For an analysis of recent Hong Kong demographics, see SIU-KAI (1982), *Society and Politics in Hong Kong*, Hong Kong, Chinese University Press.

3 For a discussion of the 1978–81 economic prosperity, see YOUNGSON A.J., (1982) *Hong Kong: Economic Growth and Policy*, Hong Kong, Oxford University Press.

4 The Hong Kong Governor's address to the Legislative Council, 5 October 1983.

5 See LLEWELLYN J., HANCOCK G., KIRST M. AND ROELOFFS K., (1982) *A Perspective on Education in Hong Kong*, Hong Kong Government Printer. One of the authors of this chapter, Michael Kirst, was also on the review panel. Note that the opening section provides a brief historical overview. For a more in-depth historical treatment of Hong Kong education, see HARRISON, B. (Ed.) (1962) *University of Hong Kong: The First Fifty Years, 1911–1961*, Hong Kong University Press.

6 Statistics from Hong Kong government, *1983 Prospects*, pp. 3–5.

7 See PARSONS M. (Ed.), (1983) *Hong Kong, 1983*, Hong Kong Government Printing Office, pp. 280–96. This annual volume includes most key Hong Kong economic statistics.

8 *Far Eastern Economic Review*, 12 March 1982, pp. 46–7.

9 *Far Eastern Economic Review*, 13 August 1982, p. 111.

10 Since one of the authors was a member of the panel, the panel's assumptions can be verified.

11 See the *Wall Street Journal*, 18 January 1984. See also the *New York Times*, 18 January 1984, p. 1.

12 Hong Kong Bank, Hong Kong Economic Report, December 1983.

13 CHAN M.K., (1983) 'Stability and prosperity in Hong Kong: The twilight of laissez-faire colonialism', *Journal of Asian Studies*, Vol. XLII, No. 3, May, pp. 589–97.

14 See *Far Eastern Economic Review*, January 1984, p. 38.

15 *Far Eastern Economic Review*, February 19, 1982, p. 45.

16 The Governor's annual address to the Legislative Council, 5 October 1983, pp. 5–6.

17 Hong Kong Government, the 1983–84 Budget Speech by the Financial Secretary, moving the Second Reading of the Appropriation Bill, 1983. See also PARSONS, M. (Ed.) 1983, *op. cit.*, pp. 284–5.

4 Nigeria: Education: The Contrast Between 1973 and 1983

M.G. Hughes
University of Birmingham, England

E.O. Fagbamiye
University of Lagos, Nigeria

Introduction

Nigeria is the largest country on the west coast of Africa and is about four times the size of the United Kingdom. Its diverse population was estimated in 1976 at over 70 million, consisting of over 250 ethnic groups distinguished by custom, tradition and language (Nwagwu, 1982). The three largest groups are the Hausas, the Yorubas and the Ibos.

Since Nigeria attained independence from Britain in 1960, great progress has been made in various sectors of the economy. The momentum of development was slowed down and in some respects temporarily reversed by the civil war of the late sixties (1967–1970), but recovery was remarkably rapid in the early seventies. The increased oil revenues which were becoming available provided the resources which enabled a widespread desire for national reconciliation and reconstruction to be given practical expression. Indeed it has been suggested that the difficulties of those times established more firmly the interdependence of the various peoples and units of the country and the need to remain united (*ibid*).

The oil boom of the early seventies made possible an unprecedented expansion of educational provision at various levels and in many parts of Nigeria. In contrast the situation ten or so years later appears to be much more precarious. The general world economic recession of the early eighties has made a particularly acute impact on the oil-dependent Nigerian economy and hence on the pace and priorities of educational advance.

It is clear that in any assessment of the changes which have occurred in the educational decision-making processes and programmes of Nigeria in the decade from, say, 1973 to 1983, the hard realities of economic constraints in the latter years of that decade are a crucial factor. Nevertheless, the impact of a contracting world economy on educational policy issues cannot easily be assessed in view of the complexity of the Nigerian situation. Quite apart from considerations related to the fact that Nigeria is a federation of nineteen states[1], with its attendant specification of state and federal responsibilities, account has to be taken of the rich diversity of traditions and loyalties within the various states and across their borders.

Even more relevant is the fact that in 1973 Nigeria was controlled by a federal military government, which had replaced the former civilian government in 1966, over a year before the beginning of the civil war.

Each of the states also had a military governor. By 1983, civilian government had again been in operation at federal and state levels for some years following transfer from military rule in 1979. With an American type presidential system of government in operation, second term elections at the federal and state levels of government took place in 1983. The profound structural changes in government that have occurred in Nigeria during the decade under review clearly have implications for educational development and serve to reinforce the thesis that the impact of the world economy of educational issues is mediated by national qualities and circumstances.

Because of the importance of the governmental change which occurred in 1979, we will consider in turn the period of military government up to 1979 and the period of civilian rule under the Second Republic from 1979 onwards.

The Military Administration and Education

On 15 January 1966 the Nigerian civil government was overthrown by a military coup d'etat. The military administration which took over the government of the country remained in control until 1979 when power was once again handed over to an elected government.

Before the military came into power in Nigeria, voluntary agencies (mainly missionary bodies) owned and controlled over 70 per cent of all primary, secondary and teacher training institutions in Nigeria. Many of these schools received grants-in-aid from government but the overall management of the institutions remained with the voluntary agencies, even though government was providing an increasingly large proportion of their funds. In the northern half of the country the situation was different since Christian missionaries had had little influence on the predominantly Muslim society. The local education authorities were well-organized and by 1967 were responsible for virtually all primary schools in existence in that part of the country.[2] The secondary schools were administered by the Ministry 'of Education in most cases.

In the southern half of the country the military coup d'etat of January 1966 was welcomed by those who wanted government to take over the schools. Most teachers anticipated better and regular salaries and uniform conditions of service for those with similar qualifications and experience. Under the voluntary agencies, teachers' salaries were often irregular and varied from one agency to the other, and in many cases conditions of service were unfavourable to teachers and often depended on the goodwill of employers. Since the military did not require electoral support to remain in power, they were more able than the politicians to disregard particular pressure groups, such as the missionary interest. They took over the schools and voted funds for education so liberally and improved the salaries and conditions of service of teachers to such an extent that opposition was muted and ineffective. The oil boom which followed the Civil War ensured that resources were readily available to support and expand the education service.

In 1973, therefore, the military government was lauded by most Nigerians for its determined policy to transform Nigeria within the shortest time possible from a background agrarian economy to an industrialized and developed one. The tool to do this 'par excellence' was education (National Policy on Education, 1977). Even though the takeover of schools was effected in a very direct military manner, the government was generally cautious in its formulation of social policies. It made extensive use of advisory bodies and valued professional expertise to a great extent. In education, for instance, the Joint Consultative Committee on Education (JCC) played a significant part in fashioning a national education policy, and there were also other groups that made inputs. Once the government was convinced of the merits of a policy proposal, it usually went ahead in military fashion to effect implementation. The points to be noted, however are, that the professionals were used extensively under the military in forward planning and that serious attempts were made to evolve educational policy in as rational manner as possible.

The Joint Consultative Committee on Education (JCC) was, and perhaps continues to be, the most important advisory committee on education. The full JCC has its membership drawn from the Federal Ministry of Education, all state ministries of education, all universities, the West African Examinations Council, the Nigerian Educational Research Council and the Nigerian Union of Teachers. In addition, there are a number of reference committees which serve as support for the full JCC. These reference committees are made up of specialists in specific disciplines. For instance, the Reference Committee on Technical Education comprises experts drawn from engineering faculties in universities, polytechnics, etc., while the Reference Committee on Educational Planning is made up of experts in educational administration and management. These reference committees discuss policy issues on specific topics and make recommendations to the full JCC which in turn examines the recommendations. The full JCC, unlike the reference committees, tries to reconcile the political point of view of government with expert advice. The civil servants and experts on this Committee try to make policy decisions in a manner that blends maximizing with satisfying as much as possible.

Thereafter, the decisions are passed on to a higher body — the National Council on Education (NCE). The NCE is made up of the Federal Minister of Education and the nineteen state commissioners for education. Once agreement is reached by this body, each state is expected to implement the decisions. Even though such decisions are purely advisory and not legally binding on any state, most states normally comply since decisions are made by consensus.

Under the military, agreement on educational policy was relatively uniform and compliance was the rule rather than the exception. A good example of this was the announcement on Free Universal Primary Education (UPE) made in 1974 by the Military Head of State, the issue having been previously agreed by the JCC. What was different in the final decision was the timing. The experts had recommended 1978 or 1979; the military government decided on 1976, which reflected the priority given to education by the military. The intention to implement the UPE policy earlier than anticipated was an important and momentous decision. Nigeria had been a party to the UNESCO declaration on African education in Addis Ababa in 1961 which called upon African governments to introduce Universal Primary Education within twenty years. It was felt that Nigeria, as a leader in Africa, was normally bound to act earlier than those that were a great deal poorer than herself, particularly in view of the improved economic situation of the early seventies as new reserves of crude oil were discovered.

The federal military government decided to finance UPE fully and even planned to make the first three years of the secondary school free from 1979. Critics of the government at the time focused on two serious flaws in the UPE policy. The first had to do with the inadequate preparation for the introduction of the scheme. Secondly, the decision to finance education fully from the federal government purse was thought to be unhealthy (Fagbamiye, 1974) for the future when government finances might not be as buoyant as they were in 1974. In answer to the first criticism, the federal government encouraged the activation of many defunct teacher training colleges and the establishment of new ones, so that by 1975 the Government was financing a total of 260 Grade II teacher training colleges all over the country. Between 1975 and 1978, 115,792 new Grade II teachers were added to the existing supply of 143,014 but the problem of teacher shortages in primary schools was not solved right up to 1979. In the euphoria of the oil boom the government merely shrugged off the second criticism concerning UPE financing and even added that by 1979 Universal Primary Education would not only be free but would also be compulsory.[3] The first three years of the secondary school were also to be free, as already noted.

The decision to introduce Universal Primary Education was not an isolated policy event. Starting from 1973 various seminars were held on a National Policy on Nigerian Education. The result of the series of seminars culminated in the National Policy on Education which was published in 1977. The emphasis of this National Policy was on education 'as an instrument par excellence for effecting national development'. Education was seen as an important area of investment in order to develop human capital. The government cancelled tuition fees in universities, polytechnics and secondary schools in the country in the 1976/77 school year as a way of encouraging educational development.

The military administration has rightly been credited with tremendous progress in various aspects of Nigerian education. For instance, at independence in 1960 there were 2,912,619 children in all primary schools and 167,460 students in all secondary level institutions including teacher training colleges in the country. By 1970, comparable figures were 3,894,539 pupils and 360,819 students in primary and secondary level institutions respectively throughout the period.[4] By 1974, however, the figures were 5,193,550 and 707,717 for primary and secondary level institutions respectively (statistics on education for various years). In the first year of UPE (1976/77), primary school enrolment rose to 8,834,730 — a figure that was 140 per cent more than five years previously.

There was also significant progress in tertiary education. In 1960, there were only two universities with a total enrolment of 1399. By 1970, there were five universities with a total enrolment of 14,531. By 1973, enrolment had jumped to 25,900 in six universities and by 1978/80, when the military left the scene, there were 57,542 students in thirteen universities with the groundwork laid for more universities — particularly technological universities. In technical education total enrolment rose to 17,485 in 1979 in twenty-three polytechnics, whereas in 1970 the number was less than a third of that figure.

Educational Finance Under the Military

The military administration was directly responsible for drawing up three national development plans — the Second, Third and Fourth National Development Plans (1970–74), (1975–80) and (1981–85) and executing the first two of the three plans. The Second National Development Plan emphasized reconstruction following the (1967–70) civil war. As Adesian (1982) has noted, the Third Plan (1975–80) paid considerable attention to education and its most outstanding feature was the introduction of UPE, the establishment of seven new universities and the takeover of the existing state universities (Ahmadu Bello University, Zaria; University of Ife; University of Benin; University of Nigeria, Nsukka) in order to ensure a steady flow of funds to all universities and facilitate the rapid and orderly production of necessary high-level manpower.

Table 4.1 shows the level of recurrent expenditure for selected years at the state and federal levels. It should be noted that primary and secondary educational have been the responsibility of states while tertiary education has always been on the concurrent legislative list. The Federal Government was, of course, more involved financially in primary education with the introduction of the UPE and the abolition of tuition fees in 1976/77, and this is reflected in the federal recurrent expenditure for that year. During the Third Plan (1975–80) N2,453,619,000 was intended to be spent on capital projects in education. The federal government was to provide 67.5 per cent while states were expected to provide the balance of that amount.

Table 4.1: Federal and State Expenditure on Education in Selected Years

Year		Recurrent Expen.	% of Total Recurrent Expen.
1972/73	All States	N159,890,000	31.33
	Federal	40,260,000	6.1
1975/76	All States	537,270,000	30.3
	Federal	240,200,000	14.1
1976/77	All States	851,880,000	38.6
	Federal	443,060,000	20.2
1977/78	All States	1,205,500,000	38.02
	Federal	238,620,000	7.7

Source: Adapted from Ndaji J. (1968–78) Financing of Education in
Nigeria Under Military Rule, Part I

Table 4.2 shows the grants to universities for the period 1972/73
to 1979/80 while Table 4.3 shows the grants in relation to universities'
request for funds. It will be noted that the federal contribution to
recurrent educational expenditure was in decline by 1977/78, the
arguments in favour of the federal financing of UPE appearing less
cogent as the economic climate began to be less favourable. The
universities also, which had been generously treated during the years
of expansion in the early seventies, were being less adequately
financed, and suffered a severe cutback in 1978/79. While enrolments
have progressively increased with the creation of new universities,
Gravenir (1983) has noted that in real terms the unit of resource (i.e.
the expenditure per student) steadily declined from 1974/75 to 1978/
79, so that in '1978/79 universities were being asked to maintain two
students with the same amount of money that was used in 1974/75 to
maintain one student'.

The fact that generous government financing for educational
development could no longer be assumed in the late 1970s was
directly related to the fact that by 1978 the oil boom had given place
to oil glut. Because of cash flow problems there were instances of the
inability of government, at federal as well as at state levels, to make
prompt payments to contractors who were executing various capital
projects. Inflation was plaguing the economy, and it was becoming
accepted that a more cautious, 'low profile', approach to public
spending was necessary in contrast to the expansionist policies of the
boom years.

It was not easy for education to adjust to the new constraints.

Table 4.2: Growth of Federal Government Grants to Universities in Relation to Growth in Enrolment 1972/73–1979/80

Year	Enrolment	Percentage increase over previous year	Percentage increase*/ decrease* based on 1970	Grants in current prices N(million)	Percentage increase/decrease over previous year	Percentage increase/decrease based on 1970**	Grants in constant prices N(million)**	Percentage increase/ decrease** over 1970
1972/73	20,204	23.6	39.0	44.0	46.6	91.3	38.8	68.7
1973/74	24,498	21.3	68.6	58.0	31.8	152.2	41.3	79.6
1974/75	27,025	10.3	86.0	83.0	43.1	260.9	52.1	126.5
1975/76	32,212	19.2	121.7	137.0	65.1	495.7	59.3	157.8
1976/77	39,902	23.9	174.6	153.0	11.7	565.7	52.1	126.5
1977/78	46,846	17.4	222.4	185.0	20.9	704.4	58.8	155.6
1978/79	49,594	5.9	245.3	159.0	−14.1	591.3	47.8	107.8
1979/80	57,542	16.0	296.0	200.0	25.7	769.6	57.0	147.8

Notes:

* computation based on composite price indices contained in Central Bank of Nigeria, Annual Report and Statement of Account 1976 and 1978 (1970–71 = 100).

** Base Year 1970/71.

Source: Gravenir F.Q. (1983) 'An assessment of the sufficiency of funds allocated to run Nigeria's university', Education and Development, 3, 1, January.

Table 4.3: *Federal Government Grants in Relation to Universities Request for Funds 1976/77–1980/81*

Year	Universities' estimated needs	Federal Government grants	Percentage shortfall
1976/77	N291,281,966	N153,000,000	47.5
1977/78	N375,168,450	N185,000,000	50.7
1978/79	N392,050,715	N158,910,000	59.5
1979/80	N411,031,076	N200,000,000	51.3
1980/81	N381,111,000	N277,000,000	27.3

Source: National Universities Commission: Annexes and Statistical Exhibits, 1980.

Taiwo (1980, p. 196), in commenting on the National Policy on Education announced by the government in 1977 after a long period of gestation, referred to it as follows: 'It was conceived during a period of buoyant economy but born in a period of tight economy which made it difficult to realize the hopes and fulfil the promises expeditiously if at all'. In practice the Third National Development Plan (1975–80) had to be scaled down, and educational expenditure did not go unscathed in the general recession. From primary education to university education the effects were becoming evident by the time the civilian administration took over in 1979.

The Second Republic and Education

On 1 October 1979 a new constitution came into operation which was intended to reverse the centralizing tendencies of the military administration. With the return of democracy, five different political parties came into existence at federal and state levels and all parties expressed a strong commitment to education, outbidding each other in the process, and having little regard in the first instance for economic realities. Hence there was a tendency towards unrealistic policies in some states and the placing of undue emphasis on the social demand approach to the development of human capital. Some states went so far as to declare education free at all levels. Some others claimed that they were after a qualitative approach rather than the quantitative education advocated in those states which had made education free at all levels. Nevertheless, it is broadly true that, in every state and regardless of which party was in power, serious efforts were made to increase educational facilities at all levels, particularly at the secondary and tertiary levels, and this in spite of very real economic difficulties. For instance, new colleges of education were opened in many states to ensure an increased supply of suitably qualified subgraduate secondary school teachers. Even though some gaps exist in the available data on new secondary schools opened since 1979, it appears that the total number of secondary schools established since 1979 is up by 60 per cent of all those in existence up to that date. For instance, Lagos state, a small but a very dynamic state, increased the number of secondary schools in the state from eighty-seven to 223 between 1978 and late 1980.

According to Adesina (1980), there were 4236 secondary schools and 2,655,774 students in the country in 1980. The increase from 1,672,866 in 1979 was more than 1 million in only one academic year. Even though enrolment figures for the 1982/83 school year are not available at the time of writing, there is no doubt that the figure would be well over the 3 million mark. This is because more provision was expected to be made for secondary education in the 1982/83 school year, since the first set of products from the six-year UPE would have been seeking secondary school places for the first time in September 1982.

In 1976, slightly over 3 million children were admitted into the primary year one. When allowance is made for wastage of say 40 per cent, at least 1.8 million would have completed primary six in June 1982. If allowance is made for 40 per cent transition rate from primary to secondary school for the country as a whole, then at least 720,000 more students would have been admitted into secondary schools in September 1982. This is a conservative estimate as some states have been operating on the basis of 100 per cent transition rate from primary to secondary school in the last three years. A realistic estimate is that the secondary school population would have topped 3.5 million in September 1982.

As was noted earlier, seven federal universities of technology, two state universities of technology and three additional polytechnics have been established since 1980. Enrolment in polytechnics has also risen from just over 17,000 in 1978 to over 26,000 in 1983. As at October 1983 there were twenty-one federal universities, including the National Open University, seven state universities, all established since 1979, one private university, giving a total of twenty nine (National Universities Commission, Lagos). The expansion in all sectors of education witnessed since 1979, achieved without a corresponding addition to resources, which were becoming increasingly strained, is impressive. A powerful incentive was that the new civilian federal and state administrations could not afford being seen to do worse than the military in the early years of their rule. The attempt to outperform each other also meant that high targets were set by all the political parties concerned.

One major problem which has become noticeable since 1979, however, has been the less uniform and more unpredictable nature of policy-making, accompanied by a less amenable attitude to expert or professional guidance. Each party has developed policies with little regard for national consciousness, such as was generally encouraged under the military regime. Consultative bodies such as the JCC are less effective, since policy recommendations can be, and are, ignored by states that so desire. Under the military, agreement on educational policy was relatively uniform and was reached without undue difficulty. Since 1979 when the civilian administrations took over, agreed recommendations have been of little consequence if they are seen as running counter to the party position. Even some of the policy decisions reached before 1979 have either been ignored or changed so drastically that a 'volte face' could be said to have occurred.

In 1977, for instance, a policy decision was taken by the JCC and later in the same year by the NCE about the need for local government education authorities to organize and administer primary education. All states started by ensuring that local governments had legislative control over primary education. But soon after the civilians took over in 1979, some states took this power out of the hands of local governments and created administrative agencies staffed with political appointees, some of whom have little academic credibility and might be regarded as being generously paid in relation to the tasks performed.

Another example is the case of the new secondary education programme which was expected to begin in all parts of the country in September 1982. Some state governments have failed to comply, even though, when the idea was initially mooted in 1976, it was generally acclaimed as a universally agreed corrective to an educational system which had tended to be irrelevant and bookish. Perhaps it has to be accepted in a federal democracy that local political considerations are liable to be paramount in relation to matters for which decision-making authority is vested at state level. Inevitably the standing of national advisory bodies such as the JCC and the NCE is called into question.

Educational Finance in the Second Republic

The pattern of spending on education did not differ much from the military period between 1979 and 1982. The sums of money voted for education were large. The Fourth Plan had projected a sum of N32 billion on all services between 1981 and 1985. Education was second on the list. In 1981, for instance, the nineteen state governments budgeted for a recurrent expenditure of N1,675,210,000 out of a total of N4,944,450,000 on all services. Education thus accounted for 33.9 per cent of the total recurrent expenditure and this compares favourably with the picture reflected in Table 4.1. The capital expenditure for the states in 1981 was N1,128,910,000 or 16.5 per cent of the total capital expenditure of N6,838,520,000 for all states. The federal government budgeted N609,760,000 and N706,950,000 for recurrent and capital expenditures on education respectively (Federation of Nigeria Budget Estimates, 1980/81). These figures represent 16.6 per cent and 7.4 per cent respectively. The total votes by the federal and state govenments, while modest, are nevertheless impressive by the standards of developing countries, and show clearly that the governments (state and federal) of Nigeria have continued to invest heavily in education, regarded as 'a panacea to eradicate illiteracy and disease and the necessary tool for achieving national development'.

The most distinctive characteristic of the Fourth Plan (1981–85) is its focus on the qualitative aspect of education. Whereas the Third Plan (1975–80) under the military was said to be quantitative, i.e. making it available to more and more, the Fourth Plan is intended to improve the quality of educated manpower at all levels and to make education for life the norm.

It has been noted that, under the military adminsistration, the world economic recession led to government inability to pay contractors promptly for completed capital projects in 1977/78, and correspondingly to some slowing down of educational expenditure. The civilian administrations which came into power in 1979 tried, without great success, to deal with inflation, but still continued to expand educational facilities. By 1982 the economic situation had steadily worsened, and harsh austerity measures were introduced. Even education, traditionally a high priority for all Nigerian governments, was seriously affected. Whereas in the past it was capital projects which suffered, from about April 1982 money was no longer available in some states to meet such recurrent expenses as teachers' salaries and fringe benefits. Schools were closed down in at least two states for almost a whole year and even federally-funded institutions suffered serious economic deprivations as well. One federal university, because of shortage of funds, had to delay the 1982/83 resumption for five weeks. Even in the first half of 1983 many teachers in at least six states had not been paid their salaries for between four and seven months.

The new secondary education programme due to be introduced in September 1982 faced serious difficulties because of the economic situation. The federal government had withdrawn from funding primary education in 1981 as a result of the new revenue allocation formula which supposedly gave more money to states without carefully matching resources and needs. If states could not cope with the demands made on them for primary and traditional secondary education early in 1982, it was unlikely they could have introduced the more expensive technical and vocational secondary programme envisaged for 1982. The Fourth National Development Plan (1981–85), which was described as too ambitious even when it was first announced in 1977/78, has had to be drastically scaled down in the face of harsh economic realities.

There are many Nigerians who now blame the civilian governments for the present economic plight of the country, and the possibility that problems have been accentuated by corrupt practices cannot be ruled out. But given the needs of the country and the demand for education in the country; and given the high rate of inflation in a country that is now highly dependent on imported goods and the unstable demands and fluctuating prices for the country's chief product (crude oil), the difficulties faced by the education system may well have been inevitable at this time.

Conclusion

The economic difficulties which have arisen as a result of the world economic recession have highlighted a number of issues. It is clear, to begin with, that the high public esteem for education makes it difficult in a young and recently re-established democracy to resist pressures for expansion even when prudent economic considerations counsel restraint. The federal nature of the country also means that different political parties may control the government at the state and federal levels. Difficulties may thus arise because of political loyalties, particularly since the maturity which makes democracy work is at a premium.

The social demand approach to educational planning is under-standably politically attractive, and the expansion in educational provision which has been achieved in economically unpropitious circumstances is quite remarkable. The far-reaching reorganization of secondary education which has been instituted to provide a better preparation for working life (Fagbamiye, 1982), though not yet fully operational in all states because of the shortage of resources, shows the vitality of a system seeking to respond to popular demand. While some will argue that the educational system has deteriorated in quality since the time when voluntary agencies administered the schools, the quantitative expansion has been impressive and much is being achieved in spite of adverse economic circumstances and some apparent deviations from financial rectitude.

It is only slowly, however, that the general public and their political leaders are coming to terms with the hard realities of financial constraints. In spite of danger signals, some state govern-ments insisted that education should be free at all levels. In present conditions this may no longer be realistic, but governments are reluctant for political reasons to introduce fees or to increase them where they were already paid.

There is some demand for privately organized and administered education, though the greater part of the population would be unable to afford to patronize private schools because of cost. Such a demand by the more prosperous has been refused in some states. On the other hand, it has to be accepted that, as long as the population of Nigeria continues to increase at a high rate of growth (currently estimated at 2.8 to 3 per cent per annum), federal and state governments are unlikely to be able to finance the full cost of a universally free educational system. This would seem to suggest that the practical answer in the foreseeable future is likely to be a public educational system administered and partly financed by government, but also financed in part by student fees, i.e. by the parents.

Finally it may be noted that, whereas the social demand approach to educational planning has hitherto been dominant in Nigeria, there are signs of increased interest in manpower forecasting and rate of return approaches. The long-term economic prospects of the country are likely to be dependent on the contribution made by men and women who have appropriate technical skills and technolo-gical expertise. There is still much to be done to ensure that there is appropriate vocational provision of tertiary education for the increas-ing numbers of students in the 1980s and nineties who will be completing their primary and secondary education as a direct result of the Universal Primary Education initiative of the seventies and the subsequent expansion of secondary education in the early eighties.

Postscript

The above chapter was jointly prepared by the authors during Dr. Fagbamiye's stay at the University of Birmingham, September-November 1983. It was thus completed before the military coup of 31 December 1983 and it was considered that it would be appropriate, and possibly more illuminating, for it to be published as it stands, without any attempt to assess the implications of the new situation. In this way it helps to place more recent developments in a historical perspective.

Notes

1 There were four regions which were sub-divided into twelve states in 1967 and these were further sub-divided into nineteen in 1976.
2 Most formal educational institutions at all levels were in the southern, predominantly Christian part of the country.
3 UPE is not yet compulsory even in 1983.
4 The 1963 Census figure was 55.6 million.

References

ADESINA, S.A. (1982) *Planning Educational Development in Nigeria*, Ibadan Board Publications.
FAGBAMIYE, E.O. (1974) 'Universal primary education in Nigeria', *Nigerian Union of Teachers Seminar/Workshop on the Universal Primary Education*, University of Lagos.
FAGBAMIYE, E.O. (1982) 'The 6-3-3-4 system of education: Implications for Nigeria', paper presented at the Fifth International Intervisitation Programme in Educational Administration, IIP82 Nigeria.
FEDERATION OF NIGERIA BUDGET ESTIMATES (1980/81), Lagos. Government Printer.
GRAVENIR, F.Q. (1983) 'An assessment of the sufficiency of funds allocated to run Nigeria's university'. *Education and Development*, 3, 1, Jan.
NATIONAL POLICY ON EDUCATION (1980) Federal Government Printer.
NATIONAL UNIVERSITIES COMMISSION, LAGOS: Annexes and Statistical Exhibits, March, 1980.
NDAGI, J.O. (1980) *Financing of Education in Nigeria Under Military Rule 1968–79 Part 1*, Zaria, Institute of Education.

NIGERIAN EDUCATIONAL RESEARCH COUNCIL, (1980) *Perspectives of Quantities and Qualities in Nigerian Education: A synthetic Report of the Baganda Seminar.*

NWAGWU, NICHOLAS A. (1982) 'The land and peoples of Nigeria', paper presented at the Fifth International Intervisitation Programme in Educational Administration, IIP82, Nigeria.

TAIWO, C.O. (1980) *The Nigerian Education System: Past, Present and Future*, Lagos Nelson (Nigeria).

5   Papua New Guinea: The Political Economy of Education

D.W. Parry
*Papua New Guinea**

Introduction

It has been suggested that the early educational policies of most newly independent nations have been dominated by political issues (Foster, 1982 p. 9). In certain respects this statement applies to Papua New Guinea which gained full independence in 1975 and embarked on a bold policy of political decentralization as a means of maintaining the unity of a nation of three million people, 85 per cent of whom, according to the 1980 Census (National Statistical Office, 1982), lived in scattered rural areas with an overall population density of only seven persons per square kilometre.

However, Papua New Guinea's early years as an independent nation have coincided with a period of international recession and inflation which, given the structure of its economy, has made the nation particularly vulnerable to external economic factors. Analysis of the impact of these factors involves consideration of a similarly innovative approach to public expenditure planning adopted by the national government shortly after independence.

Both these political and economic factors have significantly influenced the overall pace of educational development in Papua New Guinea. However, they do not entirely explain some of the more qualitative aspects of educational development since independence. Change in this area of education in Papua New Guinea, it will be argued, reflects a natural conservatism on the part of the bulk of its population which, so far at least, appears to have been consistent with

* D.W. Parry is a former staff member of the Commission for Higher Education, Papua New Guinea.

the emergence recently of a more sanguine view of the impact of education on economic development (Blaug, 1979; Levin, 1981).

Politico-Educational Institutions

Political Decentralization

Consideration of the politico-educational institutions of Papua New Guinea neatly combines discussion of what has arguably been the most radical constitutional development in Papua New Guinea since independence, namely political decentralization; and what is indisputably the most costly government department, namely education.

The reason for, the background to, and the impact of decentralization have been considered by various analysts (Allan and Hinchliffe, 1982; Ballard, 1981; Clunies-Ross, 1973; Conyers, 1976; and Griffin, 1973.) To date, however, none of these analysts has considered in detail the impact of decentralization on the development of education, although this gap should be filled shortly (Bray, 1984).

The process by which decentralization was effected, according to Ballard (1981 p. 95), was 'basic to the politics of the period from 1972' as Papua New Guinea passed through self-government and independence. Matters came to a head, however, when Bougainville, the wealthiest[1] of the nation's then eighteen districts, angered at a proposal by the Pre-independence constituent Assembly to drop the idea of provincial government from the new nation's constitution, announced the 'independence' of the Republic of the North Solomons two weeks before Papua New Guinea's own independence.

Formal resolution of this specific issue resulted in an agreement whereby the newly-named North Solomons Province remained an integral but autonomous part of Papua New Guinea. This agreement formed the basis for the *Organic Law on Provincial Government* and was the prelude to the transfer of substantial political and administrative powers to all provinces at the start of 1978. An understanding, however limited, of the process of decentralization in Papua New Guinea is essential for later developments to be adequately appreciated. Having first opposed the granting of provincial government at the time of independence, ostensibly on the grounds of cost, the national government then gave way when the economic viability of the new state was threatened and finally, almost precipitately some might argue, virtually imposed decentralization on the nation. The influence of economic factors was crucial in bringing the issue of decentralization to a head in 1975. Political considerations determined the speed with which substantial powers were then devolved to all provinces. And a combination of economic and political considerations have since influenced the extent to which decentralization has been translated in each province into real financial[2] and administrative autonomy.

Foster (1982, p. 17) has suggested that Papua New Guinea is the only newly independent country to experiment with decentralized strategies. The impact of decentralization of decision-making in education in Papua New Guinea may, therefore, have significant comparative implications.

Decentralization and Decision-Making in Education

Although Papua New Guinea has boasted a formally decentralized education system since the first Education Act of 1970, substantial powers have always been and, even under the new Education Act of 1983, will continue to be exercised by the national government.

The broad framework within which the education system in Papua New Guinea is managed is contained in the *Organic Law on Provincial Government*. This law distinguishes between 'primarily provincial subjects', which includes primary education, except curriculum (section 24); and 'concurrent subjects', which includes primary school curriculum, secondary education and research and training institutions (section 27).

A provincial legislature may make a law with respect to the former and, in so far as it is not inconsistent with any Act of the national parliament, may also make a law with respect to the latter (section 28). Teachers continue to come under the provisions of the national Teaching Service Act, subject to a guarantee as to their continued availability to provinces (section 52). Senior educational administrators and inspectors continue to be members of the national public service, assigned on a full-time basis as required to a province (section 49).

The new *Education Act of 1983* contains the detailed arrangements whereby the national and provincial governments can jointly manage the country's education system in accordance with the more general provisions of the Organic Law. In curriculum matters, for example, the new Education Act distinguishes between nationally prescribed curriculum to be taught in all schools and curriculum matters on which a provincial government may pass a law (section 28). Particularly relevant in the present context are those provisions in the Act for the production of a single education plan consisting of both national and provincial components (section 7). The provincial component may cover the establishment, maintenance and development of provincial institutions, education facilities and services in the province (section 8). Significantly, however, although these provincial components '*will*' be included within the national education plan, that plan only '*may*' recommend funding to facilitate the implementation of the provincial component (section 7: my emphasis).

Decentralization and Educational Finance

Relatively few provinces have been able to benefit significantly from the internal provincial revenue generating provisions contained in the Organic Law. For the majority of provinces, over 90 per cent of their revenue comes directly from the national government in one of three forms (Bray, 1982a, p. 8). Firstly there are conditional grants, tied to new developments in education; and secondly grants intended to equalize educational provision between provinces. Both these are relatively small in absolute terms but largely determine the general direction of educational development in a province.

The third and largest component of provincial revenue, constituting 78 per cent of the total revenue of all provinces, are the Minimum Unconditional Grants. The size of these grants is based on the maintenance of various services, including education, at the level immediately prior to the attainment of full financial autonomy for those financially autonomous provinces (see note 2). For these provinces the total grant, including that element for education, may be used entirely as the province determines. For partially autonomous provinces, that element of the unconditional grant included for education, must be spent on educational provision, although the province has discretion as to specifically what form that provision should take.

To date, no detailed analysis is available to indicate how much, if any, additional money is allocated to education by provinces than that received in the ways indicated above from the national government. However, as noted earlier, internally generated revenue, with the notable exception of the North Solomons and, to a lesser extent, East New Britain provinces, is extremely limited: nor can provinces negotiate formal overseas aid arrangements. On the basis of plans so far produced, however, few provinces appear to be likely to implement major quantitative or qualitative changes involving substantial increases in education spending.

The Impact of Political Decentralization on Education in Papua New Guinea

In summary, responsibility for long-term planning in education at the pre-tertiary level is a *shared responsibility* between national and provincial governments. *Provinces* have control of staff establishments, selection policies, enrolments and the general administration of education in the province. *National* control is, however, still exercised in major curriculum matters, over the terms and conditions of teachers, over examinations and certification and over all post-secondary education. The legislative power retained by the national government ensures its continued dominance over the qualitative aspects of the education system. And even in those areas where provinces have substantial legislative powers, these may be eroded in practice by both a lack of administrative and planning skills at the provincial level (Bray, 1982a, p. 16) and by the complex arrangements for financing educational provision described earlier which allows the national government to continue to maintain a significant influence on the overall size and general development of the education system.

Whilst acknowledging, therefore, the fact of political decentralization, the development of education in post-independence Papua New Guinea is still largely influenced by nationally determined aims and objectives and nationally provided funding. This is so even at the pre-tertiary level where much greater political and administrative responsibility is legally in the hands of the provinces. At the post secondary level, national control is overriding, substantially affected, however, by the division of responsibility for the nation's more than 60 post-secondary institutions between 14 different government ministries. An examination of the resources available and the distinctive budgetary process developed in Papua New Guinea since independence will reveal the extent of this control.

Economic Resources and Policies

External Factors Influencing the Papua New Guinea Economy

External economic factors have dominated government expenditure plans for the last decade. Three major factors can be highlighted. Between self-government in 1973 and the first full year of independence in 1976, *mineral fuels and lubricants* increased as a proportion of the nation's total import bill from 5 per cent to 14 per cent — an increase of 180 per cent. By 1981, these same items accounted for 21 per cent of the total import bill — a rise of over 300 per cent in less than 10 years (National Planning Office, 1982 p. 28).

At the time of self-government, untied *Australian aid* to the country was by itself equivalent to internally generated revenue (Papua New Guinea, 1982, p. 513). Official government policy since achieving independence has been gradually, and according to an agreed formula, to reduce the country's reliance on Australian aid (Central Planning Office, 1976, p. 15). Although a good deal has been achieved in this respect since independence, untied grants from the Australian government constituted approximately 27 per cent of estimated government revenue in 1983, with other aid and concessional borrowing accounting for an additional 5 per cent. Internally raised revenue still only accounted for half of total revenue in 1983 (Papua New Guinea, 1982, p. 509).

Dominating Papua New Guinea's internal source of revenue are the earnings from its substantial *mineral resources*. The increasing significance of this sector of the economy is indicated in Table 5.1.

Table 5.1:   Export of Merchandise 1977–1981 (extract only)

Export Sectors	1977	1978	1979	1980	1981
Mining	38%	44%	50%	50%	55%
Non-mining	62%	56%	50%	50%	45%

Figures rounded.
Source: National Planning Office, 1982, p. 24.

Not only is Papua New Guinea dependent on foreign expertise and capital for the exploitation of these mineral resources, it is also at the mercy of fluctuating prices on the world market for the resulting

Table 5.2: Major Export commodity Prices (extract only)

Commodity	Units	Annual 1970s average price	Annual Prices			Projected 1980s average price	Percentage change from 1970s	Percentage of 1981 exports by value
			1980	1981	1982			
Copper	US¢/lb.	119	110	80	68	93	−22	24
Gold	US$/oz.	273	625	478	350	323	+18	30
Coffee	kina/tonne	2654	2743	1650	1922	1690	−36	21

Figures rounded.
Source: National Planning Office, 1982, p. 18.

exports. Table 5.2 indicates the extent of these fluctuations.

Strategies to reduce oil consumption; a long-term aid agreement with Australia; and the establishment of a Mineral Stabilization Fund, all constitute attempts to protect Papua New Guinea against sudden and dramatic, externally influenced changes. The impact of such changes on the budget in general and the government's response in respect of education is demonstrated by an analysis of the annual National Public Expenditure Plan proposals which have provided the strategic budgetary framework for Papua New Guinea's development since independence.

The National Public Expenditure Plan

The National Public Expenditure Plan (NPEP) system was designed as the major policy-making tool to direct national government expenditure towards agreed goals of national development. A detailed analysis of the NPEP process is contained in Allan and Hinchliffe (1982). In summary, the NPEP system established a four-year, rolling plan period of operation; an explicit set of criteria in the form of 'strategic objectives'[3] as the basis for resource allocation; a consistent procedure for the evaluation of new expenditure proposals; and, decentralization notwithstanding, a firm control over major public expenditure decisions at the national level.

A ceiling was placed on all spending under policies existing in 1977 and any new developments requiring additional funds since that date have been scrutinized in the light of the strategic objectives referred to above. Total government expenditure was planned to grow at a modest 3 per cent per annum, a growth rate decided explicitly in the light of fluctuations in world market prices for the principal export commodities and the level of Australian aid (National Planning Office 1978a, p. 17).

Acceptance of this growth rate was reiterated annually until the 1982–85 NPEP which, noting the doubling of oil prices during 1980 and 1981 and the fall in commodity prices, planned for no growth in public expenditure in 1982 and 1983 and a 1 per cent growth only in 1984 (National Planning Office, 1981b, p. 14). The 1983–86 NPEP planned a 5 per cent reduction in total public expenditure; a 4 per cent cut in grants to provinces and a 10 per cent cut in the number of public servants (National Planning Office, 1982, p. 4). In addition, during 1983, a reduction in the previously agreed rate of decline of Australian aid was negotiated.

National Policy Guidelines and Financial Provision for
Education in Post-Independence Papua New Guinea

A year after independence the national government published a
document outlining its national development strategy for the new
nation. With regard to education the document emphasized that the
goal of universal primary education for as many people as possible
were to be objectives central to the government's policies (Central
Planning Office, 1979, p. 79). At the post-primary level the document
emphasized the link between formal education and employment and
noted continuing and possibly conflicting, popular pressure for this
level of education.

Funds for all aspects of primary education were planned to
increase by 5 per cent annually from 1979 onwards (National
Planning Office, 1981, p. 19). Even in 1982, when the gloomiest
budget since Independence was brought down, room was still found
for the allocation of K2.6m (over 10 per cent of all available new
funds) to finance a free primary education scheme, in addition to the
various ongoing programmes aimed at expanding educational provision. This specific scheme was abandoned the following year by a
newly-elected government but once again, despite a 5 per cent cut in
public spending, continuing high priority was to be given to education which, after agriculture, was to receive the largest proportion (16
per cent) of new government expenditure (National Planning Office,
1982, p. 6). Since independence, between 17 and 19 per cent of the
nation's annual budget has been allocated for education. Approximately 60 per cent of this has been for primary and secondary
education and the remainder for colleges and the two universities in
the post-secondary sector (Commission for Higher Education,
1983a).

Issues in Education in Papua New Guinea Since Independence

Balanced Educational Growth

The general proposals for the development of education envisaged in
the National Development Strategy were purportedly based on the
Education Department's own long-delayed National Education Plan
for the period 1976 to 1980 (Department of Education, 1976.) The

Plan, in the words of its authors, aimed for 'balanced educational growth' which involved attempting to reconcile the sometimes conflicting pressures of *expansion, suitability and quality.*

One definition of a good plan is that it is actually implemented and its targets met. On the basis of actual performance Papua New Guinea's independence Education Plan has to be judged a failure. In reality, the Plan was doomed almost before the document left the press. 'Budgetary constraints have already prevented the achievement of planned targets' concluded the first NPEP document for the period 1978–1981 (National Planning Office, 1978a, p. 50). Despite this, the Plan's enrolment targets for 1980 were incorporated in that NPEP document!

The prudent recommendation of the authors of the Plan that a review of progress towards implementation of the plan be undertaken midway through the plan period was by 1978 an urgent necessity. The conclusions of the review committee, appointed in 1978 when compared with those of the 1976 Plan, were more sober in their targets for *expansion* in every area of education; more realistic in their assessment of what constituted a *suitable* education; and more conservative in their judgment as to what determined *quality* in education (IASER, 1979).

At the heart of the debate on the speed and direction of educational change in Papua New Guinea was a desire on the part of the national government both to expand and equalize educational provision at the lower, less expensive levels of education, but not at the risk of endangering standards; and at the more expensive post-secondary level, to expand the range of vocational training to allow the replacement of costly, high-level overseas manpower with qual-

Table 5.3: Enrolment targets and actual performance 1975–1982

Primary Level Entry	1975	1980	1982
1 Original grade 1 enrolment targets	—	75,050	85,482
2 Revised grade 1 enrolment targets	—	64,019	73,934
3 Actual enrolments	51,963	62,165	68,548

Sources:
1   Department of Education, 1976.
2   IASER 1978.
3   Department of Education '*Staffing and Enrolment Statistics*' for relevant years.

ified Papua New Guineans, but not at the risk of producing large numbers of educated unemployed.

Expansion

The review committee acknowledged that the planned 3 per cent annual growth rate in the economy was insufficient to enable the original enrolment targets for *primary* education to be met. They were, therefore, revised downwards as indicated in table 5.3. At the *secondary level* a policy dilemma was recognized; whether to contain expansion as closely as possible to projected manpower needs or to go as far as possible in meeting the social demand for secondary education. Once again, a downwards revision was recommended by the review committee with the implications indicated in table 5.4. At both the primary and secondary levels, economic factors were used to justify reductions in enrolment targets despite evidence of popular demand at the secondary level. Targets at neither level have been adhered to, with grade 1 enrolments less, and grade 7 enrolments more than their respective targets. At both levels the trends emerging so far show planned and actual enrolments moving further apart.

Table 5.4: Enrolment targets and actual performance 1975–1982

Secondary Level Entry	1975	1980	1982
1 Original grade 7 enrolment targets	—	13,320	—
2 Revised grade 7 enrolment targets	—	11,656	12,296
3 Actual enrolments	10,189	12,098	13,021

Sources:
As for table 5.3.

One important dimension of the debate on expansion has been the issue of equality of provision. All educational planning documents have stressed the need to reduce inequality between provinces in terms of the proportion of the school-age population in school and between male and female enrolments. Recent evidence suggests that progress has been made on both these fronts, in particular with regard to the former at the primary level (Bray, 1982a, p. 4) and with regard to the latter at both the primary and secondary levels in those provinces which have adopted affirmative action policies towards female enrolments (Weeks, 1983).

Absolute increases in enrolments have been significant with a 32 per cent increase in enrolments at the grade 1 level between 1975 and 1982; and a 28 per cent increase at the grade 7 level for the period. These increases reflect a financial commitment on the part of the national government to make funds available through the NPEP as indicated earlier to expand both *primary and secondary level education* with approximately 75 per cent of all new 'tied' funds on education outside the university sector being allocated for quantitative expansion since 1978. In that provinces can decide whether to spend their (much larger) untied funds on quantitative or qualitative developments in education, the overall enrolment figures quoted above also reflect a community belief that education remains an attractive private 'investment' in Papua New Guinea (Conroy, 1970 and 1972; Carrier, 1981). The first national manpower assessment provided clear evidence of this, concluding that an analysis of earning ratios for national workers showed that 'every additional year of schooling is separately rewarded' (National Planning Office, 1981a, p. 32).

What has been significant in terms of any meaningful progress towards the goal of *universal primary education*, however, has been the steady decline in enrolments in, and as a consequence, output from primary teachers' colleges, a sector of education totally under national control. The figures in table 5.5 speak for themselves!

Table 5.5: Enrolment targets and actual performance 1975–1982

Primary Teachers' Colleges	1975	1980	1982
1 Original enrolment targets	—	2650	3200
2 Revised enrolment targets	—	2102	2540
3 Actual enrolments	1990	1708	1660

Sources:
As for table 5.3.

Suitability

The authors of the Education Plan and the members of the Review Committee stressed the importance of a suitable or relevant education. This was initially used to support the renaming of *primary schools* which became known as community schools, emphasizing the terminal, self-contained nature of education at this level. A community school education was described in terms of 'what it does that is peculiarly appropriate in its own setting and might be inappropriate elsewhere' (Department of Education, 1976, p. 15).

A note of caution was sounded, however, right from the start, Whilst reorientation of primary education was necessary, attempts to reorient primary education were not to be allowed to out-run the conditions for its success. A fundamental condition was an adequate supply of teachers which, as we have seen, although planned for, has not eventuated. The Review Committee noted that in seeking views of people throughout the country it was clear that there was a general belief that 'the home, the village and the clan could inculcate cultural values better than could the school' (IASER, 1978, p. 2). The populist ground-swell, it was suggested, was not for the status quo, and education was seen as the key to change and mobility.

Accordingly, the national government has maintained control over core curriculum matters viz English, maths, science and more recently community life (formerly social science), and only relatively small amounts have been allocated through the NPEP process to make a reality of community-based education as originally envisaged. Alternatives have been proposed (Kemmelfield, 1972; Kopi, 1979) but a radical reorientation of primary schools in Papua New Guinea has yet to eventuate.

Perhaps the most significant and sustained attempt by the national government to provide more relevant education has been at the *secondary level* with the Secondary Schools Community Extension Project (SSCEP). This was a pilot project, trialled in five high schools and funded through the NPEP for the years 1978 to 1982. The aims of the project were to reduce urban drift; enable students to contribute to rural development through self-employment; deinstitutionalize education; integrate the learning of practical and intellectual skills; and improve the teaching and curriculum development skills of teachers (Currin, 1979).

Formal evaluation of this project is still in the early stages. It is interesting to note, however, that in 'selling' the project, it has been necessary to demonstrate that job placements of graduates from these programmes have improved and academic results have been maintained (Cummings, 1983). This highlights the dilemma recognized by the authors of the Education Plan who defined a suitable secondary education as one in which the curriculum was intended to meet the needs of students proceeding to higher education and/or employment *as well as* those returning to their communities (Department of Education, 1976, p. 124).

D.W. Parry

At the *post-secondary level,* a suitable education has been interpreted as meaning one which meets national manpower requirements (National Planning Office 1978a, p. 80). This has involved
a significant degree of expansion in technical education, targets
which have more than been achieved (see table 5.6), involving the
introduction of numerous new pre-employment technical training
programmes.

Table 5.6:   Enrolment targets and actual performance 1975–1982

Pre-employment technical training	1975	1980	1982
1 Original enrolment targets	—	4500	—
2 Revised enrolment targets	—	3000	3000
3 Actual enrolments	1125	3778	3131

Sources:
As for table 5.3.

Apart from the expansion of technical education, post-secondary
education, including the universities, has been assumed to have had
(more than) sufficient capacity to meet overall manpower needs.
What was required, it was argued, was a reallocation of resources
(National Planning Office, 1978b, p. 105) and/or the building up of
certain disciplines at the expense of others. The degree of success of
this policy can be seen in the analysis of output in selected fields for
the period 1978 to 1982 in table 5.7, showing a clear trend in favour of
commerical business administration and secretarial training and engineering and technical trade training.

Table 5.7:   Output in selected fields 1978–1982 (percentage of total)

Field of study	1978	1982	1978–1982
Agriculture, fisheries and forestry	9	8	9
Commercial, business administration and secretarial	17	22	20
Education and teacher training	37	28	31
Engineering and technical trade	23	31	28
Other	14	11	12
TOTAL	100	100	100

Source: Commission for Higher Education, 1983b.

Quality

Possibly the most contentious issue in education in post-independence Papua New Guinea has been the issue of quality. Concern for quality has rarely, however, been based on agreement as to what is meant by the term, although this has not necessarily prevented firm recommendations for action to maintain or improve quality.

For the authors of the Education Plan 'quality' was a key concept which required that 'adequate measures (be) taken to preserve and where necessary to improve the quality of teaching and learning'. (Department of Education, 1976, p. 6). This depended on the number and quality of teachers and was the basis for that plan's recommendations for a substantial increase in places for both pre-service and in-service teacher education and training. The committee reviewing the Education Plan, using standardized psychological tests as one proxy for quality, concluded that standards had declined and quoted 'widespread and genuine concern about quality' (IASER, 1978, p. 4). The cause of the drop in standards, it was argued, was the policy of using English as the medium of instruction in a situation where most teachers were not first language English speakers. Assuming that the language policy was to be retained, the solution to the problem lay once again in improved pre-service and in service teacher education and training. In addition, it was argued, improvement in quality at both the primary and secondary levels of education involved systematically 'tilting' the curriculum in the direction of greater competency in basic subjects such as language, number, science and the social sciences (*ibid*, pp. 33 and 48).

The outworkings of this concern are to be seen in, amongst other developments, the allocation of resources to maths and English curriculum development, and the establishment in 1978 of a Standards Division within the Department of Education responsible for curriculum, materials development, educational measurement, guidance and inspections.

Concern for quality continued to be expressed, however, and led to the appointment by the Minister for Education in early 1981 of a Committee of Enquiry into educational standards (Committee of Enquiry, 1981). This Committee undertook a wide-ranging review of the quality, efficiency and management of education at all levels. The report of the Committee, containing as it did some 200 recommendations, constituted the most thorough enquiry into education in Papua New Guinea since the Committee of Review in 1978. It did not, however, provide estimates of the financial implications of its recommendations as the 1978 Review had done and gave little indication as to priorities. Both factors have limited the extent to which the report has been translated into a policy document for politicians to take decisions on and bureaucrats to implement. One further limitation was the lack of an adequate definition of the terms quality or standards, beyond the comment that 'at the present stage in the nation's development ... it is within the domain of the formal economy, and the education ladder leading to it, that standards must be set and measured in relation to the outside world in which Papua New Guinea exists and competes' (Committee of Enquiry, 1981, p. 22).

What has been a feature of the three major reports referred to has been the relatively conservative approach to the development of education in Papua New Guinea reflected in them, largely due to a concern for the maintenance of quality, however defined, a caution generally echoed in the provincial education plans so far produced.

As a result, despite a well documented and well publicized attempt to raise awareness about the issue (Anderson, 1981), non-formal education, for example, remains largely neglected apart from a small component in the first of three major World Bank loans for education in Papua New Guinea. And, despite experiments at provincial level over the years with a variety of selection methods for entry into secondary schools based on equity and other non-academic criteria, a growing number of provinces are now reverting to a more conservative and easily operated and understood selection system based entirely on academic merit (Bray, 1982b, p. 165).

Conclusion

In 1975, when Papua New Guinea gained independence, decentralization was the dominant political issue; self-reliance the key economic objective; and education the biggest item of government spending. Virtually the same could be said of the country eight years after independence.

At the time of writing, the national government is debating legislation to facilitate the suspension of provincial governments under certain circumstances in the light of what, at the national level at least, is seen as a history of mismanagement, incompetence and corruption at the provincial level. In 1975 internal revenue accounted for just over 51 per cent of total government revenue. The 1984 Budget recently debated in Parliament estimated that internal revenue will account for just under 55 per cent of total government revenue. And the national Education Department continues to be the biggest item of government spending.

In many respects, education has weathered the political and economic difficulties which have faced the country since independence remarkably well. The new Education Act of 1983 represents the only serious attempt by a national department really to come to grips with the issue of decentralization in the light of the provisions of the Organic Law on Provincial Government. The reality of control at the national level in most major decisions concerning the overall size and quality education provision nevertheless remains.

National control is reinforced by the financial provisions for provincial government and the NPEP process. Only a few provinces are financially autonomous; even fewer are able to generate significant internal revenue; and those that are remain, by the nature of their major revenue earners, subject to the same world commodity price fluctuations influencing the national budget.

The NPEP process initially allowed the national government to freeze the status quo. By monopolizing the acquisition of overseas aid and determining the allocation of this and other newly available, internally generated funds since 1978, the national government has continued to control the majority of the financial resources required to enable new or existing educational policies to be effectively implemented. Education has, as a result, secured significant new funds through two World Bank loans and a third about to be signed — the largest to date. The reasons for the priority accorded to education and the type of educational provision that has resulted can be attributed partly to the political and economic constraints which have already been outlined and partly to values apparent within, but not exclusive to, Papua New Guinea.

In the years immediately preceding self-government and independence, Ivan Illich and Paulo Freire respectively were invited to speak at major public seminars held in Papua New Guinea. They advocated radical alternatives to the formal education system which had been implanted in the country by the colonial Australian administration and spoke to an articulate, receptive and educated elite on to whose shoulders the leadership of the new nation would be placed (Freire, 1975; Illich, 1973).

In the event, however, it was the cautious pragmatism advocated by a third pre-independence visitor, Philip Foster, that has been most reflected in the educational development of post-independence Papua New Guinea (Foster, 1975).

Papua New Guineans have been quick to see not only the substantial private returns to education but also the limits to those returns. This has been reflected, for example, in the gradual change from popular pressure for primary to pressure for secondary education as employer requirements have change, and in a reluctance to experiment with educational forms whose 'investment potential' was unproven. This has, in turn, enabled the national government's approach to universal primary education to be gradual rather than precipitate and allowed resources to be devoted at the same time to the maintenance of quality and more equal educational provision between different provinces and between male and female students at both the primary and secondary levels where responsibility for education has been shared by the national and provincial governments.

These sentiments have also, to date at least, lent support to the allocation by the national government of substantial resources to a post-secondary education system offering an impressive range and level of programmes, the rationale for which has been the need to produce indigenous, high-level manpower. The recent establishment of a Commission for Higher Education to advise government on the future development of the post-secondary sector may, however, reflect a desire on the part of the national government to rethink this policy in so far as it has resulted in an elitist, high-cost and underutilized post-secondary education system. Indeed, one interpretation of this development is that the national government, faced with externally influenced economic constraints and continuing internal demands from provinces for funds for education, plans to divert resources from higher education to other levels of education in order to make meaningful progress towards UPE and the inevitable consequential expansion of secondary education.

The impact of externally influenced economic factors cannot be ignored when considering the development of education in post-independence Papua New Guinea. These factors have, however, been mediated by the relatively cautious but politically acceptable approach adopted by the national govenment to the development of education.

In attempting to predict future developments it is necessary to speculate on the extent to which the national government can continue to maintain its substantial control over the allocation of financial resources in the face of increasing pressure from provincial governments for more funds and fewer 'strings'.

Rowley (1971) has suggested that decentralization which may be necessary at the time of independence, or in the period following it, may be short-lived. With the growth of national cohesion, decentralization of education may come to be decided on educational grounds. But the trend, Rowley argued in 1971, had been in the other direction on account of political reasons although educational reasons required decentralization. This article has attempted to show how the conflicting forces of political decentralization and national control of the economy have influenced the development of education in Papua New Guinea since independence.

On balance, it would seem that Foster's suggestion of the dominance of political issues in the early educational policies of most newly independent nations applies to Papua New Guinea. Certainly it is within the context of the balance between national and provincial governments that the educational issues of expansion, suitability and quality will continue to have to be worked out.

Final judgment on the impact of decentralization on education in Papua New Guinea cannot yet be made, but any attempt to evaluate the process should take care to distinguish between political rhetoric and economic reality.

Notes

1 Exports out of Kieta, Bougainville's main port, accounted for 60 per cent of all Papua New Guinea's exports in 1975 (National Statistical Office 1982, p. 121).

2 Provinces may be divided between those with full financial autonomy, *i.e.* having almost total discretion as to how to spend money disbursed to them by the national government; and those with partial autonomy, *i.e.* having discretion in respect of part only of the money disbursed by the national government, the remainder being 'tied' to certain activities. In 1983, the following eight provinces were fully autonomous: East New Britain; Eastern Highlands; East Sepik, Madang; Morobe; New Ireland; North Solomons and West New Britain.

3 The nine strategic objectives, and the proportion of new funds to be allocated to each objective, are listed below:

Rural welfare	20%	Training and Participation	5%
Helping Less Developed Areas	9%	Urban Management	2%
General Welfare	7%	Effective Administration	11%

D.W. Parry

Economic Production   35% Environmental Management 1%
Food and Nutrition   4% [Fiscal Commission]   5%
Source: (National Planning Office 1978 (b) p. 11)
The Fiscal Commission is intended to alleviate possible short-term
problems as Provinces move towards full financial autonomy. Com-
mercial projects amounting to a further 1 per cent should be added.

References

ALLAN, W. and HINCHLIFFE, K. (1982). *Planning, Policy Analysis and Public Spending: Theory and the Papua New Guinea Practice*, Aldershot, Gower.
ANDERSON, B.D. (Ed.) (1981). *The Right to Learn: The Neglect of Non-Formal Education*, Port Moresby, Hebamo Press.
ANDERSON, LASCELLES and WINDHAM, D.M. (Eds.) (1982). *Education and Development: Issues in the Analysis and Planning of Post-colonial Societies*. Lexington Books, D.C. Heath and Company.
AXLINE, A. (1983). 'Financial Foundations of Provincial Policy Making in Papua New Guinea', Unpublished IASER Seminar paper, November, (Mimeo).
BALLARD, J.A. (Ed.) (1981). *Policy Making in a New State: Papua New Guinea 1972–1977*, St Lucia, University of Queensland.
BLAUG, M. (1979). 'The quality of population in developing countries with particular reference to education and training', in HAUSER, P.M. (Ed.) (1979) pp. 361–402.
BRAMMALL, J. and MAY, R.J. (Eds.) (1975). 'Education in Melanesia'. Report of the 8th Waigani Seminar, May 1974. University of Papua New Guinea.
BRAY, M. (1982a). 'Decentralisation and educational inequalities', Paper delivered at the 1982 Waigani Seminar on 'The Eight Aims and the National Goals', University of Papua New Guinea.
BRAY, M. (1982b). 'High school selection policies in 1981. The impact of decentralisation', *Papua New Guinea Journal of Education*, Vol. 18, No. 2, pp. 155–167.
BRAY, M. (1983). 'The politics of free education in Papua New Guinea', *International Journal of Educational Development*, Vol. 2, No. 3, pp. 281–287.
BRAY, M. (1984). *Educational Planning in a Decentralised System: The Papua New Guinea Experience*, University of Papua New Guinea Press.
CARRIER, J.G. (1981). 'Education as investment: Education, economy and society on Ponam Island', *Papua New Guinea Journal of Education*, Vol. 17, No. 1, pp. 18–38.
CENTRAL PLANNING OFFICE (1976). *National Development Strategy: Papua New Guinea Government White Paper*, Port Moresby Government Printer.
CLUNIES-ROSS, A. (1973). 'Secession without tears', in CLUNIES-ROSS, A.

and LANGMORE, J. (Eds.) (1973), pp. 131–138.

CLUNIES-ROSS, A. and LANGMORE, J. (Eds.) (1973). *Alternative Strategies for Papua New Guinea*, Melbourne, Oxford University Press.

COMMISSION FOR HIGHER EDUCATION (1983a). 'Summary of an Analysis of Annual Appropriations for Schools, Colleges and Universities, 1978–1983' (Mimeo).

COMMISSION FOR HIGHER EDUCATION (1983b). 'Summary of a Statistical Analysis of Graduates from various sectors of Higher Education: 1978–1982' (Mimeo).

COMMITTEE OF ENQUIRY (1981). *In Search of Standards*. Report into Educational Standards established by the Minister for Education. Port Moresby, Hebamo Press.

CONROY, J.D. (1970). 'The private demand for education in New Guinea: Consumption or investment?' *Economic Record*, 46 (116) pp. 497–516.

CONROY, J.D. (1972). 'Education and the economy of New Guinea', in SELLECK, R.J.W. (Ed.) (1973), pp. 228–263.

CONYERS, D. (1976). 'The Provincial Government debate'. IASER Monograph 2. Port Moresby.

CUMMINGS, R. (1983). 'Major findings of the evaluation study of SSCEP', Department of Education Seminar, October, (Mimeo).

CURRIN, C. (1979). 'Curriculum development in SSCEP: A general report for 1979', Department of Education, Port Moresby (Mimeo).

DEPARTMENT OF EDUCATION (1975). 'Education staffing and enrolment statistics: National Education System'.

DEPARTMENT OF EDUCATION (1976). *Education Plan 1976–1980*, Port Moresby, Government Printer.

DEPARTMENT OF EDUCATION (1980). 'Education staffing and enrolment statistics: National Education System'.

DEPARTMENT OF EDUCATION (1982). 'Education staffing and enrolment statistics: National Education System'.

FOSTER, P.J. (1975). 'Dilemmas of education development: What we might learn from the past', in BRAMMALL, J. and MAY, R. (Eds.) pp. 15–38.

FOSTER, P.J. (1982). 'The educational policies of postcolonial states', in ANDERSON and LASCELLES (Eds.), pp. 3–25.

FREIRE, P. (1975). 'Liberation through literacy', in BRAMMALL, J. and MAY, R. (Eds.) pp. 245–249.

GRIFFIN, J. (1973). 'Movements for separation and secession', in CLUNIES-ROSS, A. and LANGMORE, J. (Eds.), pp. 131–138.

HAUSER, P.M. (Ed.) (1979). *World Population and Development: Challenges and Prospects*, Syracuse University Press.

ILLICH, I. (1973). 'A "convivial society" for Melanesia?' in MAY, R.J. (Ed.).

INSTITUTE OF APPLIED SOCIAL and ECONOMIC RESEARCH (1979). *National Education Strategy: Papua New Guinea Education Plan Review and Proposals*, Port Moresby, Hebamo Press.

KEMMELFIELD, G. (1972). 'A community-based education system: A proposal', University of Papua New Guinea, *Education Research Unit Report No. 3*, Port Moresby.

KOPI, S. (1979). 'Alternative systems of education', *POINT*, 1, pp. 96–113.

LEVIN, H.M. (1981). 'The identity crisis of educational planning', *Harvard Educational Review*, Vol. 51, No. 1, pp. 85–93.

MAY, R.J. (Ed.) (1973). 'Priorities in Melanesian Development'. Report of the 6th Waigani Seminar, May 1972, University of Papua New Guinea.

NATIONAL PLANNING OFFICE (1978a). *The National Public Expenditure Plan 1978–1982*, Port Moresby, Government Printer.

NATIONAL PLANNING OFFICE (1978b). *The National Public Expenditure Plan 1979–1982*, Port Moresby, Government Printer.

NATIONAL PLANNING OFFICE (1981a). *National Manpower Assessment: 1979–1990*, Port Moresby, Government Printer.

NATIONAL PLANNING OFFICE (1981b). *The National Public Expenditure Plan 1982–1985*, Port Moresby, Government Printer.

NATIONAL PLANNING OFFICE (1982). *The National Public Expenditure Plan 1983–1986*, Port Moresby, Government Printer.

NATIONAL STATISTICAL OFFICE (1982). *Papua New Guinea Summary of Statistics: 1979*, Port Moresby, Government Printer.

NATIONAL STATISTICAL OFFICE (1983). *1980 Population Census Pre-Release: Summary of Final Figures*, Port Moresby.

PAPUA NEW GUINEA (1982). *Estimates of Revenue and Expenditure for the Year Ending 31st December 1983*, Port Moresby, Government Printer.

ROWLEY, C.D. (1971). 'The politics of educational planning in developing countries', *IIEP Pamphlet no. 15, Fundamentals of Educational Planning*, Paris.

SELLECK, R.J.W. (Ed.) (1973). *Melbourne Studies in Education*, Melbourne University Press.

WEEKS, S.G. (1983). 'Male and Female Enrolment Rates at Various Levels of Education' (Mimeo).

6 The People's Republic of China: Education during the World Recession: The Paradox of Expansion

Stanley Rosen
University of Southern California,
USA

Contrary to the experiences of most other LDCs, China has weathered the international recession surprisingly well. One need not subscribe fully to former West German Chancellor Helmut Schmidt's comment that 'no country has been able to escape from the crisis except the People's Republic of China' (China Reconstructs, 1983), to acknowledge that China has increased its trade surplus and lent dollars internationally, that industry and agriculture have both achieved rapid growth. As *The Economist* observed (1983b), this is a 'remarkable' performance in a world slump.

Nor, apparently, has the recession restricted China's educational funding. In fact, investment in education has steadily increased in recent years. Although China still lags behind most of the world in state investment for education (see below), there are powerful voices in the country urging further educational investment. Thus, whereas in 1978 expenses on education totalled only 5.9 per cent of the state budget, by 1982 this figure had risen to 10 per cent (Daily Report, 1983a). At the outset, therefore, one confronts some compelling evidence that the state of the world economy has had little impact on the Chinese economy, and still less on Chinese educational policy.

Ironically, the period of the international recession (1979–1982) *has* coincided with a major reorientation in Chinese domestic and foreign policy, including startling changes in educational policy, but these policy shifts have been induced by changes in the domestic rather than the international environment. Simply stated, the death of

105

Mao Zedong in September 1976 and the political demise of his radical supporters less than a month later — including those now referred to as the 'Gang of Four' — has substantially altered the Chinese developmental strategy. The longstanding debate over the transition to socialism between those who stressed the primacy of rapid economic development and those who viewed the development of socialism as much in redistributive as in developmental terms has, for the present, been decided in favor of the 'developmentalists'. The familiar Chinese model that rested on a mass-based mobilization approach, with a commitment to policies of self-reliance and socialist and egalitarian distribution, to periodic attacks on status barriers, and the use of institutionalized measures designed to systematically break down the role differences between mental and manual labor, has seemingly been rejected (Eckstein, 1978).

The post-Mao leadership has embarked on a developmental strategy that closely resembles what analysts in the west have described as interdependence. Although the Maoist goal of self-reliance remains enshrined in current rhetoric, it has now been operationalized to accommodate some very 'un-Maoist' modifications (Wu, 1981). For example, President Li Xiannian, then a vice-premier in charge of economic planning, told an American trade delegation a decade ago that China was not, and would never be, interested in foreign capital to develop its economy, not even its oil reserves. Today, China is anxiously searching for massive amounts of foreign capital and advanced technology to modernize its industry and develop its natural resources. In addition to joint equity ventures, coproduction, compensation trade, and processing, China has announced its readiness to allow foreign companies, under certain conditions, to establish wholly owned subsidiaries in coastal cities like Shanghai and Tianjin (Parks, 1983; Stepanek, 1982).

Indeed, China's position in the world economy has changed markedly in recent years. For example, two-way foreign trade has leaped from US $14.7 billion in 1977 to $42.2 billion in 1983, with projections calling for $160 billion by the end of the century. But China's influence in the international market, while potentially great, is as yet unrealized. China's exports amount to only a small fraction of domestic output, and a tiny part of world trade. With almost 25 per cent of the world's population, and 5 per cent of the world's economic output, China accounts for only about 1 per cent of the world's trade (Davie and Carver, 1982, p. 20; JPRS, 1983a and 1983d; China Business Review, 1984.)

China's potential role — and its susceptibility to future fluctuations in the international market — stems from a uniqueness among centrally planned economies and third world states that has produced a mutual attraction between the middle kingdom and the West. Unlike the Soviet bloc countries which trade heavily among themselves, China's trade with other tightly planned economies accounts for less than 10 per cent of its total trade, while over 65 per cent of its trade is with the developed capitalist world. Moreover, since only about 0.5 per cent of all Western imports come from China, there is considerable potential for the country to benefit from its greatest comparative advantage — large numbers of low-wage laborers — to expand and develop its export lines (Davie and Carver, 1982, p. 35; Yuan *et al*, 1980). Export earnings and direct foreign investment will allow China to import the high technology and management skills necessary to fuel its modernization.

For the West, China represents a potential market of one billion (with 200 million urban customers) and an industrial economy badly in need of modern equipment. Foreign firms have engaged in coproduction — the source of 91 per cent of the total foreign investment in China in 1981 — primarily in the hopes that it will lead to further penetration of this huge import market. Foreign banks have been enthusiastic in offering the Chinese loans since, unlike many third world countries, China is not burdened with heavy international debts, has a favorable balance of payments, substantial reserves of gold and foreign exchange, a budget close to balance, and little foreign indebtedness (Shirk, 1984; Stepanek, 1982)

There are pitfalls, however, in this rosy picture of potential mutual benefit between China and the West. Since China has only recently become more active in the world economy — the country began to welcome foreign joint ventures in July 1979 and joined the IMF and World Bank in the spring of 1980 — it has been trying to procure massive amounts of foreign investment to fuel long-term developmental plans during the height of the recession. This has presented China's pragmatic leaders with the difficult task of simultaneously avoiding the ravages of the recession, attracting direct foreign investment, and placating a domestic opposition which is scrutinizing the 'open door' policy for possible 'betrayals of socialist self-reliance'. Thus far, through a policy of fiscal conservatism, China has been relatively successful in handling the recession. Because China has not been heavily dependent on foreign trade, has little commerical debt, was not much affected by high interest rates, and was insulated by a large domestic market, the World Bank concluded in its recent annual study, it has come through the recession with encouraging resilience (World Development Report, 1983, p. 2; Manning, 1983, p. 118).

Indeed, China has used the recession to its own economic advantage. While the Bank of China has lent billions of dollars abroad (to Hong Kong enterprises and through participation in many Euro-currency syndicated loans), the Chinese government has informed foreign investors that the country is too poor and interest rates too high for China to support its development effort with high-priced foreign loans. While maintaining one of the lowest debt-service ratios in the world, China has steadily built up its foreign-currency reserves, from US$2.6 billion (not counting gold holdings) at the end of 1980 to US$5 billion in 1981, then more than doubling to US $14.5 billion by the end of 1983 (Delfs, 1983b; China Business Review, 1983 and 1984; Economist, 1983a; Stepanek, 1982).

On the other hand, foreigners have been reluctant to invest directly in joint venture projects — the favored choice of Beijing officials who want to maximize the importation of high technology and Western management knowhow — because of uncertainties over Chinese regulations, bureaucratic obstacles, the government's protection of its domestic market, Chinese reluctance to assist investment projects with high interest loans or other forms of credit, and so forth. Of the US$16.2 billion in foreign capital used from 1979 through 1982, only about 10 per cent had been in the form of direct investment. In 1982, fresh foreign investment dropped by more than 50 per cent to under US$50 million. In response, China introduced new joint venture and taxation laws in 1983 and Chinese officials planned to obtain pledges of foreign investment worth US$3 billion. But foreign investment has continued to run below plan (Parks, 1983; MacDougall, 1982; Stepanek, 1982; Economist, 1983c and 1984). Realizing that, under current economic conditions, only low wages, low prices, and the promise of the China market will attract foreign investors and customers to China, the leadership has begun to clarify and liberalize its joint venture regulations. However, this has fueled the opposition of those vested interests in China who are ill-placed to benefit from the open door to the West. Any further concessions to encourage Western investment will increase the reaction of those referred to by one analyst as the 'communist coalition' (Shirk, 1984; Parks, 1983).

The outcome of this debate over China's foreign economic relations is likely to have profound implications for the country's educational development strategy. For example, China will be unable to absorb Western technology and investments usefully without a vast improvement in the educational and managerial level of its labor force. Whatever the ultimate mix between self-reliance and inter-dependence, however, the post-Mao leadership, by allowing educational investment to move to the forefront as an important agenda issue, has altered the terms of the debate over education.

The new legitimacy accorded education as a factor in economic development has already had a major impact in Chinese social, political and economic life. The increasing state investment cited earlier is only one of many highly visible changes to appear. In their pursuit of the 'Four Modernizations' — modernization of industry, agriculture, science and technology, and national defense — China's leaders have introduced policies more favorable to the country's intelligentsia than at any time since the establishment of the People's Republic in 1949. Mental workers have, since 1979, been relieved of their status as members of the 'petty bourgeoisie' and have joined manual workers as part of the 'laboring people', thus greatly alleviating the necessity to transform their world outlook. Intellectuals, backed by prominent party leaders, have begun to argue that education is a productive force rather than a part of the superstructure, and therefore a prime sector for investment dollars. Although this view is by no means universally accepted — one recent article summarizing the debate over education as productive force or superstructure distinguished five major positions on this issue — such open academic contention marks a significant shift from previous analyses which viewed education almost solely in terms of consumption, and as an instrument of class struggle and the dictatorship of the proletariat (Li Kejing, 1980).

Perhaps the most striking departure, given their trials and tribulations in post-1949 China, has been the willingness of educators to speak out and compete directly with other sectors — such as heavy industry — for a larger share of the state budget. Although details regarding the substance or even the process of inner party and governmental budget debates are not available for public scrutiny, the arguments of the educators appear at some length in specialized journals (*People's Education, Educational Research,* social science journals and journals of various universities and teachers' colleges). Moreover, advocates for greater educational funding have embraced the ideas of some controversial Western theorists, most notably Theodore W. Schultz's human capital theory, linking this approach to communist ideology (Yang and Yang, 1982).

One fascinating aspect of the current debates is the division within the academic community over priority sectors for educational investment between those favoring concentrated funding for the country's best schools and those supporting increased attention to basic primary and junior high school education. This discussion is closely related to debates over the role of education in modernization and will be discussed briefly below.

Educational Structure, Funding and Policy in Post-Mao China: An Overview

China's present educational structure cannot yet be considered congruent with the nation's ambitious modernization plans. In spite of strong measures to neutralize its egalitarian thrust, the Cultural Revolution (1966–76) legacy has not been fully eradicated. Its presence continues in several forms. For example, objecting to a tracking system as inherently unequal, China's 'radicals' had turned all secondary schools into comprehensive schools and greatly expanded enrolments. The secondary school enrolment ratio went from 16 per cent in 1965 to over 50 per cent by 1977 (14.4 million enrolled to over 68 million enrolled). Under the current policy of retrenchment, by 1982 the number of secondary school students had been reduced to just over 45 million, but they were still unevenly distributed. Whereas 31 per cent of all secondary school students were in vocational (including agricultural middle) schooling in 1965, as late as 1981 the equivalent figure was just 0.99 per cent (Rosen, 1984). Equally serious, according to China's present 'moderate' leadership, was the decline in educational standards during the Cultural Revolution as the radicals virtually eliminated postgraduate education, promotion up the educational ladder by competitive examination, and differences in school quality (Pepper, 1978; Unger, 1982).

Given the radical reforms of the Cultural Revolution, the post-Mao leadership have determined that a mere restoration of the educational structure of the mid-1960s, while necessary, would not be sufficient to repair the damage. The system that has been erected, therefore, has a much stronger emphasis on quality and hierarchy than ever before. It is geared to the early discovery and training of talented students in 'keypoint' schools; it provides a fast track for the brightest students, who can move up the keypoint system from primary school all the way through university. For the very best, there are increasing possibilities for postgraduate education, both in China and abroad.

China now operates under a 6-3-3-4 system.[1] As indicated above, however, tracking exists at every level. The most desirable schools are the keypoint schools. These schools are provided with additional funding, are allocated the best teachers, and recruit the brightest students. Since promotion to the next higher level of schooling is based almost exclusively on examination performance, there is intense competition, particularly from primary school graduation on up, to test into a keypoint school. The most crucial examination is for university entrance. Because of the large number of senior high graduates and the limited number of university places, only a small percentage of high school graduates can be enrolled (in 1979 it reached its nadir of 4.08 per cent; it has steadily risen to 12.6 per cent in 1983) (Rosen, 1983).

The university entrance examination is particularly crucial because, in what has become a very tight job market, university graduates are part of the state employment allocation system; they have guaranteed jobs awaiting them. High school graduates — including those in regular, academic schools as well as vocational school — are no longer guaranteed employment. Under recent policy reforms, such graduates are encouraged to find jobs themselves, normally in the less desirable collective and private sectors of the economy.[2] At least in part because vocational schooling has yet to be effectively tied into the job market, students have continued to crowd into academic track schools and take their chances on making it to university, commonly opting for vocational education only if they cannot test into the academic stream.

Attendance at a keypoint senior high greatly enhances one's chances for university enrolment. The best of these schools — usually run by provincial or municipal education bureaus — send well over 90 per cent of their graduates to university. Less well-endowed keypoints, such as those run by municipal districts or counties, have much lower success rates, with ordinary (non-keypoint) schools sending very few of their graduates on to university. In 1980, of the almost 120,000 regular high schools, 5200 were keypoints, but only 700 were chosen for priority funding and development.

At the university level as well, qualitative distinctions exist. For example, of the 1.15 million students in full-time universities in 1982 (enrolment ratio below 2 per cent), just over 225,000 were in short-cycle two-or three-year programs. Of China's 715 universities, ninety-four have been designated national keypoints and are managed directly by the Ministry of Education or another central ministry. Among these, twenty-six have been selected for special assistance from the World Bank. More recently, in May 1984, ten of the country's best universities were singled out as 'research universities', to be given the highest funding priority (Rosen, 1984b).

The financial responsibility for education and training in China is divided among the central ministries, provinces, municipalities, counties, communes, brigades, enterprises, parents and adult students. More specifically, the central government's contribution to education in 1979 was estimated at 64 per cent of the total, with local governments, brigades and enterprises, and so forth contributing 28 per cent, and families contributing 8 per cent (World Bank, 1983, pp. 180–5). The World Bank estimated total public expenditure on education in China in 1979 to be 3.1 per cent of GNP, placing China below the median percentage (3.9 per cent) of eighty-two developing countries on which the Bank has information. In developed countries the percentage has been around 5.7 per cent. Central government expenditure on education as a percentage of total expenditure has also been low, at 6.6 per cent (in 1979) compared to 15.1 per cent in other LDCs and 15.6 per cent in developed countries, although this figure had risen to 10 per cent by 1982. China has shifted more of the cost of education, particularly at the primary and secondary levels, to local authorities and communities than is common in other socialist or developing countries. State investment in education, in accordance with the current emphasis on quality and hierarchy, has favored urban over rural schools, university over primary and secondary education, and keypoint schools over ordinary schools. For example, China spends a higher percentage (30 per cent) of educational expenditures on tertiary education than do other LDCs or the OECD countries. Likewise, unit costs of primary and secondary education as a percentage of GNP per capita are low in China compared with those in other countries, while those in higher education are high. At primary and secondary level, the variations in educational spending are substantial. Since so much of education at this level has to be locally funded, it is clear that the degree of urbanization and industrialization of a locality, the level of agricultural prosperity, as well as the value placed on education, will play a major role in determining the availability and quality of educational opportunities.

Education and Economic Development: The Debate in China

China's intellectuals have made rapid strides in recent years. Under Mao Zedong the role of educators and the formal, institutionalized educational structure had been, at best, somewhat ambiguous. The school was merely one agency in society — and not necessarily the most important agency — imparting learning. Learning also took place in factories, on farms, in the streets, through mass campaigns and so forth. The suspension of regular school work for weeks and months at a time so that teachers and students could engage in labor and production, or could join the masses in political-ideological campaigns, was an accepted procedure under what has been called the Maoist 'revolutionary model' of education (Chen, 1981; Hawkins, 1974; Starr, 1979). The present Chinese leadership has gone on record as vehement opponents of this revolutionary model. Their own statements stress the crucial importance of the institutionalized educational system and the initiative of educational workers in fostering economic development. Deng Xiaoping has taken a direct interest in education, particularly in science and technology, and has frequently stressed the close relationship between educational development and modernization. Hu Yaobang, the Secretary-General of the Chinese Communist Party, has publicly supported the efforts of educators who lobby for additional state investment. Given such high-level encouragement, funds allocated to the Ministry of Education have steadily increased over the past few years, with virtually no viewpoints opposing investment in education granted publication in the official press and openly circulated journals.

In spite of such support for the concept of intellectual investment, public educational spending in China is unlikely to match the allocations commonly found in the developed countries. There are a number of reasons for this pessimistic assessment, for the reluctance of both central and local governments to increase rapidly their funds allocated to education. Most fundamental is the continued widespread belief, particularly among economists, that investment in education is consumptive. Although virtually every issue of the leading education journals contains at least one article on the underlying importance of education in economic development, and leading educators have access to such authoritative party organs as *People's Daily* and *Red Flag*, economists generally remain unconvinced. They routinely note that 'non-productive investments in culture, education, scientific research, health, sports ... municipal public utilities

... housing and other investments that are directly related to people's life' must be guaranteed. But they also argue that the improvement in the standard of living must be built on the foundation of developing production, otherwise both 'will be adversely affected' (JPRS, 1983b, and f).

A striking instance of the differing perspectives of economists and educators can be seen by examining their alternate assessments of the reasons for the Japanese 'economic miracle'. In a recent article in *Red Flag*, one of China's foremost educators traced Japan's success to its educational development strategy, to the fact that funds for education in Japan rose tenfold from the 1950s to the 1970s, and that in 1971 educational funding amounted to 20.4 per cent of the state budget, ranking first in the world (China's allocation to education that year was 4.5 per cent). He concluded by citing a Japanese white paper which argued that 'investment in education is an unusually important investment in production' (JPRS, 1983e).

A different view was offered by a leading economist — now president of the Chinese Academy of Social Sciences — who visited Japan on an inspection tour in 1978. In a speech to be used as internal study material, he cited seven factors in Japan's economic development, but ignored completely the role of the Japanese educational system. His only mention of education, in fact, came in a section entitled 'the seamy side', when he discussed the difficulty university graduates have in gaining employment[3] (JPRS, 1983c).

This view of education also tends to prevail in most Chinese provinces, where education is often considered to be consumer and welfare work. Education departments are seldom able to find bureaucratic allies to support their demands for increased investment. Even among those who are willing to concede that education may be a productive investment, there is reluctance to use scarce funds on an enterprise which has such a long cyclic period. Returns on educational investment commonly take even longer than the construction of some infrastructures (for example, transport and power systems). Particularly in poorer provinces and counties, the necessity for a better educated cadre force has been met by the indiscriminate transfer of teachers from the education front to other work, at best a short-term solution (Li, 1981). One problem often singled out in the press is the widespread diversion of funds — allocated by the province to prefectural, municipal or county education bureaus — to other projects, ranging from the building of factories (which are considered 'productive') to the erection of cadre housing.

It is not just the localities, however, that balk at using investment funds for education. The center as well has given capital construction in the economic sector priority of investment, arguing that educational development should take place gradually to match the pace of economic development. A recent *People's Daily* editorial sought to convince the localities to spend their money on education rather than on construction projects which are outside the national plan. Communes and brigades were told not to consider raising funds for schools as an 'irrational burden'; factories, mines, enterprises and institutions were also urged not to view such fund-raising as an 'extra burden'. As the editorial put it, since education is a cause of the whole society, various social forces should play their role. To expect the state to increase investment in education too much or too fast was viewed as 'unrealistic' (Daily Report, 1983b).

Although there is little space to elaborate, there are important reasons why the center has recently become particularly concerned with local investment decisions. As part of the government's reform program, decentralized economic decision-making has replaced state control of the allocation of economic resources. New policies which treat industrial enterprises as autonomous entities, which can retain profits for their own use, have led to the growth of so-called extra-budgetary funds equivalent to 60 per cent of the total state budget, most of which are under the control of individual enterprises and local administrative units. Bank loans have supplemented the growing amount of investment funds beyond the center's direct control. Local administrations often invest in heavy industry projects which compete with central government projects for scarce raw materials and support services, as well as strain energy and transport sectors. At least some of China's leaders would gladly countenance a drop in the heavy industry growth rate — which zoomed to 9.9 per cent in 1982 instead of the planned 1 per cent increase, hit 13 per cent in 1983 against a target of 4 per cent, and registered 11.7 per cent in the first six months of 1984, more than twice the 5 per cent planned — if the localities would invest more of these excess funds in non-industrial construction, such as education, housing and culture. From the vantage point of local administrators, however, heavy-industry projects are not only prestigious, but may be rational responses to ensure reliable local sources of supply for critical intermediate industrial products. What central planners view as wasteful and inefficient duplication may be locally necessary to compensate for an irrational and inefficient supply and transportation system. Thus, in the local competition for these vast extra-budgetary funds, weaker sectors like education usually lose out

(Delfs, 1983a and 1984; Naughton, 1983; Economist, 1984).

If increased educational spending has faced resistance at various administrative levels in favor of more 'productive' investments, the educators themselves have differed over the priorities to which educational investment funds might be put. At least two basic groups can be discerned. Both groups share the view that educational investment cannot wait for economic prosperity, but rather is the foundation for such prosperity. Likewise, both groups realize that modernization requires the rapid training of scientific and technological personnel. However, one group supports priority investment at the top of the educational pyramid and the other group emphasizes the necessity of starting from the bottom. Interestingly, both groups base their arguments in part on the successful experiences of the developed countries. Each group has been represented by some of the country's most prominent intellectuals and has had access to such widely circulated authoritative publications as *People's Daily*.

The first group — apparently centered around retired university presidents — has advocated the concentration of resources in the fifty or so strongest universities in the country. These schools would expand their recruitment of undergraduate and graduate students, become more actively involved in scientific research and, to guarantee priority funding, would be listed among the key construction projects of the state. The result by 1990, according to the advocates, would be the production of several hundred thousand high-quality undergraduates, tens of thousands of Master's candidates, several thousand PhD candidates, and numerous professorial-level leading scholars in all fields. In addition to providing personnel for the economic construction of the 1990s, these schools would train excellent teachers for the remaining universities and lay a solid foundation for the development of higher education (JPRS, 1983h).

The second group — centered around Fei Xiaotong and his colleagues on the Chinese People's Political Consultative Conference, a united front organization representing intellectuals and other social forces — has argued that the most efficient means of training more professionally competent personnel is to raise the cultural level of those at the basic level. As Fei puts it, 'attention should be paid to developing intellectual resources throughout the country rather than cultivating a small number of elites. The raising of standards should be based on popularization'. Fei and his group have been especially upset by the negative side effects associated with the keypoint primary and secondary schools. On the one hand, they argue, these schools can never train enough personnel to meet the needs of a modernized nation; on the other hand, the concentration of attention and funding in these schools has demoralized the majority of students attending the ordinary schools, who find themselves generally ignored. This has contributed to relatively high (for China) drop-out rates and a low educational standard for those who graduate. Fei's group argues that the keypoint system has contributed to the 'new illiteracy'. The 1982 census revealed that China still has 235 million illiterate and semi-illiterate people, almost one person in four. The solution this group favors is the abolition of keypoint primary and secondary schools, and the enforcement of compulsory primary education (JPRS, 1983g).

Given sufficient funding, it would not be impossible to satisfy both groups. Under current conditions, however, neither group's objective is likely to be fully achieved. Although all three of the most urgent issues facing Chinese education — (i) universalization of primary education; (ii) structural reform of secondary education and the development of vocational-technical education; (iii) speeding up the expansion of higher education — are receiving national attention, the solutions offered assume minimal investment by the central government. For example, there has been a great emphasis on promoting basic education, with plans for universal primary education by 1985 in districts relatively well developed economically and educationally, and a target date of 1990 of less developed districts. These plans, however, require much of the investment to come from local governments and the recipients themselves. Those advocating a stress on basic education want the central government to allocate more national funds for this project. At the secondary level, because there is little money to invest in vocational or technical education, academic track high schools are being shut down but not replaced by any alternatives. Finally, while China's keypoint higher institutions are becoming more autonomous in such areas as enrollment decisions, budgeting, and administration, and seem to be getting the bulk of the investment funds available for universities, expansion at the tertiary level has primarily been in non-formal education, such as TV and correspondence universities. Enrollment in full-time universities is expected to increase by 53 per cent between 1983–87 (in part because of the expansion of two- and three-year programs); however, the increase in non-formal college education will be 270 per cent over the same period (Ogden, 1982; Pepper, 1983; Rosen, 1984a).

Conclusion

The period of the international recession has coincided with a fairly substantial increase in the allocation of governmental funds to education. Although the level of state investment in education still lags behind most other nations, a shift in socio-economic developmental strategy in the post-Mao years has meant a higher status for intellectuals and a recognition that educational and economic development are interrelated. The realignment in developmental strategy has also impelled the Chinese government to play a more active role in the world economy. To date, however, the Chinese have been cautious both in their dealings with the capitalist world economy and their support for higher spending levels for education. The view still held by many that education is a consumptive drain rather than a productive investment has not been fashioned under the impact of the world recession; rather, it is a legacy of China's earlier developmental model.

Since China's 'open door' policy has only recently been implemented and lobbyists in the educational sector have finally been accorded the overdue legitimacy necessary to argue their case in public, it perhaps is more interesting to speculate about the *future* influence of world economic fluctuations on the Chinese economy and the educational system. It seems clear that China's increasing demand for advanced technology and its dependence on the world market for its export trade will make the country more vulnerable to future market conditions. The Chinese have already admitted that protectionism has caused them some problems, that high interest rates have obstructed their planned use of foreign capital, and that price cuts in petroleum and coal — which together account for a quarter of total exports by value — have hurt. Moreover, there seems to be a real question over whether developed-country markets for such export items as textiles and shoes have become saturated in the light of industrial-country unemployment and protectionism. Since the ASEAN countries, as well as South Korea and Taiwan, already have substantial market access, it is debatable whether China, moving increasingly into the international arena, can find the markets which justify external orientation in the 1980s (Rowley, 1983; China Reconstructs, 1983; Delfs, 1983b).

Given these uncertainties, how dependent is the Chinese educational system on foreign economic policy? First, the foregoing argument has presented the Chinese educational system as essentially bifurcated, with a relatively small elite sector receiving a disproportionate share of state funding and a much larger basic-level sector which is compelled to rely heavily on local investment and self-reliance. For example, almost half of China's one million primary and middle schools have work-study programs to raise money; factories, mines, and communes often fund their own vocational and agricultural middle school programs; school construction and repair depend almost solely on money contributed locally, and so forth (Li, 1982; Beijing Review, 1982; China News Analysis, 1982). China's role in the world economy is unlikely to alter this self-reliance at the base of the educational pyramid.

A greater impact might be expected at the elite level. The World Bank's first China loan, signed in November 1981, called for US $200m in expenditures for instruments, computer equipment, and training at twenty-six key universities. Moreover, although China has received only US$235m in International Development Association (IDA) commitments, World Bank lending to China is expected to increase dramatically to a total of US$2.4 billion in 1984/85. From 1978 to the end of 1982, 12,000 Chinese had studied abroad at state expense, mostly in the natural sciences; over 3500 have already returned to China (Delfs, 1983c; Gong, 1982). But it is far too early to determine how effective this investment in advanced science and technology education has been; for example, there are mixed reports concerning the role the returned Chinese students and scholars have been allowed to play. One gets a strong sense, however, that the spectre of domestic opposition will continue to compel China's advocates of the open door to tread lightly, that those pressing for greater educational spending will have difficulty prevailing over a strong heavy industry lobby, and that educators pushing for more funds from the center for basic education are likely to be disappointed. The wild card in all this, of course, is Deng Xiaoping. Deng has become so closely associated with the open door strategy and the importance of investment in knowledge that many Chinese will only be convinced that the current policies are permanent if they can be sustained after their architect has passed on.

Notes

1   Since secondary schooling was reduced to a combined five years of junior-senior high, there has been a staggered return to a 3–3 system, with the highest quality schools adding a third year of senior high first. The process should be completed by 1985.

Stanley Rosen

2   An exception to this are the graduates of secondary specialized schools, who are also provided jobs. Entrance to these schools is also considered very desirable. Currently, these schools recruit both junior and senior high graduates; eventually, only junior high graduates will be recruited. In 1981, only 2 per cent of all secondary school students were in such schools.

3   In a more recent work this economist, Ma Hong, did refer to the necessity to increase investment in science and education, but still relegated this sector to a lower priority than other sectors of the economy. See Ma Hong, 1983.

References

BEIJING REVIEW (1982). *Tailoring Education to Fit China*, 18 October, pp. 23–8.

CHEN, T. HSI-EN (1981). *Chinese Education Since 1949: Academic and Revolutionary Models*, New York, Pergamon Press.

CHINA BUSINESS REVIEW, (1983). *The Benefits of Fiscal Conservatism*, January–February, pp. 48–9.

CHINA BUSINESS REVIEW (1984). January–February, p. 53.

CHINA NEWS ANALYSIS (1982). *Education, 1980–82*, 30 July, pp. 1–8.

CHINA RECONSTRUCTS (1983). *Amid World Slump, China's Economy Grows*, August, pp. 32–5.

DAILY REPORT — CHINA (1983a). *Statistics Reveal Changes in Last Four Years*, 20 June, pp. K 20–23 [Xinhua, June 14].

DAILY REPORT — CHINA (1983b). *Raise Funds Through Various Channels to Run Schools, Accelerate the Introduction of Universal Primary Education*, 31 August, pp. K 16–18 [Renmin ribao, August 27].

DAVIE, J.L. AND CARVER, D. W. (1982). 'China's international trade and finance', *China Under the Four Modernizations, Part 2*, Washington, Joint Economic Committee, Congress of the United States, pp. 19–14.

DELFS, R. (1983a). 'Return to the centre', *Far Eastern Economic Review*, 23 June, pp. 56–8.

DELFS, R. (1983b). 'The spectre of inflation', *Far Eastern Economic Review*, 4 August, pp. 40–1.

DELFS, R. (1983c). 'All those great expectations are still only a modest aid flow', *Far Eastern Economic Review*, 29 September, pp. 94–5.

DELFS, R. (1984). 'Balancing the books', *Far Eastern Economic Review*, 16 August, p. 62.

ECKSTEIN, A. (1978). 'The Chinese development model', *Chinese Economy Post-Mao, Vol. 1, Policy and Performance*, Washington, Joint Economic Committee, Congress of the United States, pp. 80–114.

ECONOMIST (1983a). *At War Over China*, 26 February, p. 84.

ECONOMIST (1983b). *Best-Laid Plans*, 12 march, pp. 75–6.

ECONOMIST (1983c). *Slow Road: Investment in China*, 2 April, p. 77–8.

ECONOMIST (1984). *China's Lop-Sided Investment*, 21 January, p. 71.

GONG YUAN (1982). 'Chinese Studying abroad', *Beijing Review*, 6 December, pp. 25–7.

HAWKINS J.N. (1974). *Mao Tse-tung and Education*, Hamden, The Shoestring Press.

JOINT PUBLICATIONS RESEARCH SERVICE (JPRS) (1983a). 'Jingji Guanli' on Improving Foreign Trade, No. 83486, 18 May, pp. 49–56 [Jingji Guanli, 5 March].

JOINT PUBLICATIONS RESEARCH SERVICE (JPRS) (1983b). Journal on New Path of Economic Construction, No. 83595, 2 June, pp. 5–16 [Zhongguo Jingji Wenti, 20 March].

JOINT PUBLICATIONS RESEARCH SERVICE (JPRS) (1983c). Noted Chinese Economist Discusses Japan's Economic Development. No. 83693, 16 June, pp. 129–44 [The Seventies (Hong Kong), February 1983].

JOINT PUBLICATIONS RESEARCH SERVICE (JPRS) (1983d). New Characteristics of China's Foreign Trade. No. 83780, 28 June, p. 123 [Jingji ribao, 11 May].

JOINT PUBLICATIONS RESEARCH SERVICE (JPRS) (1983e). Attention to knowledge Must Go Hand in Hand With Attention to Education. No. 83808, 1 July, pp. 1–7 [Red Flag, 16 April].

JOINT PUBLICATIONS RESEARCH SERVICE (JPRS) (1983f). Jinji Yanjiu on Country's Production, Consumption. No. 83836, 7 July, pp. 1–15 [Jingji Yanjiu, 20 May].

JOINT PUBLICATIONS RESEARCH SERVICE (JPRS) (1983g). Fei Xiaotong Urges Development of Education. No. 83966, 25 July, pp. 19–21 [Renmin ribao, 25 June].

JOINT PUBLICATIONS RESEARCH SERVICE (JPRS) (1983h). Accelerate Building of Key Universities. No 84047, 4 August, pp. 5–6 [Renmin ribao, 11 June].

LI KEJING. (1980). 'Is education a superstructure or a productive force?', *Social Sciences in China*, September, pp. 16–25.

LI YINING. (1981). 'The role of education in economic growth', *Social Sciences in China*. June, pp. 66–84.

LI YONGZENG. (1982). 'Work-study programmes in primary and middle schools', *Beijing Review*. 8 November, pp. 21–4.

MA HONG. (1983). *New Strategy for China's Economy, Beijing*, New World Press, chapters 1 and 2.

MACDOUGALL, C. (1982). 'Policy changes in China's foreign trade since the death of Mao, 1976–1980', in GRAY, J. and WHITE, G. (Eds) *China's New Development Strategy*, New York, Academic Press, pp. 149–71.

MANNING, R. (1983). 'Up north, down south', *Far Eastern Economic Review*, 29 September, pp. 117–8.

NAUGHTON, B. (1983). 'State investment in post-Mao China: The decline of central control', paper prepared for the Social Science Research Council Conference on Policy Implementation in Post-Mao China, Ohio State University, 20–24 June.

OGDEN, S. (1982). 'The politics of higher education in the PRC', *Chinese Law and Government*, 14, 2, summer.

PARKS, M. (1983). 'Critics blast China policy on investing', *Los Angeles Times*, 24 October.

PEPPER, S. (1983). *China's Universities: Post-Mao Enrolment Policies and Their Impact on the Structure of Secondary Education*, Ann Arbor, Michigan, Center for Chinese Studies, University of Michigan.

Stanley Rosen

PEPPER, S. (1978). 'Education and revolution: The 'Chinese model' revisited', *Asian Survey*, 18, 9, pp. 847–90.
ROSEN, S. (1983). 'Restoring keypoint secondary schools in post-Mao China: The politics of competition and educational quality, 1978–1983', paper prepared for the Social Science Research Council Conference on Policy Implementation in Post-Mao China, Ohio State University, 20–24 June.
ROSEN, S. (1984a). 'New directions in secondary schooling', in MAYHOE, R. (Ed.) *Contemporary Chinese Education*, London, Croom Helm.
ROSEN, S. (1984b). 'Recentralization, decentralization, and rationalization: Deng Xiaoping's bifurcated educational policy', paper prepared for the American Political Science Association Annual Meeting, Washington, D.C., 29 August–2 September.
ROWLEY, A. (1983). 'The upturn's down side', *Far Eastern Economic Review*. 4 August, pp. 38–40.
SHIRK, S.L. (1984). 'The domestic political dimensions of China's foreign economic relations', in Kim, S.S. (Ed.) *China and the World: Chinese Foreign Policy in the Post-Mao Era*, Boulder, Co, Westview Press, pp. 57–80.
STARR, J.B. (1979). *Continuing the Revolution: The Political Thought of Mao*. Princeton, Princeton University Press.
STEPANEK, J.B. (1982). 'Direct investment in China', *The China Business Review*, September–October, pp. 20–7.
UNGER, J. (1982). *Education Under Mao: Class and Competition in Canton Schools, 1960–1980*, New York, Columbia University Press.
WORLD BANK. (1983). *China: Socialist Economic Development, Volume 3, The Social Sectors*. Washington, D.C.
WORLD DEVELOPMENT REPORT 1983, New York: Oxford University Press.
WU, F.W.Y. (1981). 'From self-reliance to interdependence? Developmental strategy and foreign economic policy in post-Mao China', *Modern China*, October, pp. 445–82.
YANG B. and YANG H. (1982). 'An analysis of "human capital theory"', *Educational Research* (Jiaoyu Yanjiu), January, pp. 75–80 (in Chinese).
YUAN W., DAI L. and WANG L. (1980). 'International division of labor and China's economic relations with foreign countries', *Social Sciences in China*, March, pp. 22–47.

7   The United States of America: The Educational Policy Consequences of an Economically Uncertain Future

James W. Guthrie
*University of California, Berkeley,
USA*

Introduction

The United States has recently emerged from a remarkably unsettling economic period. Beginning in 1976, inflation rates climbed to levels unprecedented in this century. This was followed immediately by a dismal two-year recession, relief from which did not begin to appear until 1983. The recent roller coaster of an inflationary high followed by a recessionary low triggered substantial uncertainty and a high measure of national self doubt regarding the American economy. However, somewhat contrary to what might be expected, the economic downturn and subsequent uncertainty did not impose dramatic damage upon the financial base of American schools. Rather, education in many of the fifty states virtually stayed even financially and during the subsequent recovery has begun to regain the revenue ground that was previously eroded. However, even if not having an immediate debilitating effect upon the day-to-day financial operation of education programs, recent economic instability has catalyzed an extensive national effort to make America's education systems more productive. Morever, a public policy link between schooling and the economy has re-emerged and is guiding a nationwide reform effort aimed at achieving academic excellence. This chapter analyzes the evolution of these conditions. In order better to establish a context for this explanation, we begin with a brief description of recent United States economic conditions, summarize current US educa-

tion policy-making arrangements, and then undertake a discussion
of education policy trends.

The United States Economy: 1976–1982

In the period from 1976 to 1982, the United States' economy was
deeply troubled. Federal fiscal and monetary policies, coupled with a
six-fold petroleum price increase, contributed to a staggering double
digit inflation rate of 61.2 per cent over the seven-year period. Abrupt
1981 reversals in federal spending patterns, by the national government, and Federal Reserve Board, restraints on the creation of
money and uncommonly high interest rates on borrowing, subsequently triggered a two year-long recession, which lasted until
recovery began to surge in the third quarter of 1983.[1]

Economic instability and fiscal contraction affected public agencies as well as the private sector. Prior to the late 1970s, all three levels
of American government experienced substantial and sustained expansion. As can be seen from Figure 7.1, in 1929 total federal, state
and local government spending equaled 10 per cent of Gross National
Product (GNP). By 1975, the comparable figure was 35 per cent. By
1976, however, the proportion of GNP accounted for by total
government spending began to decline.

*Figure 7.1:   Spending as a function of gross national product, by level of
government, 1929–1979*

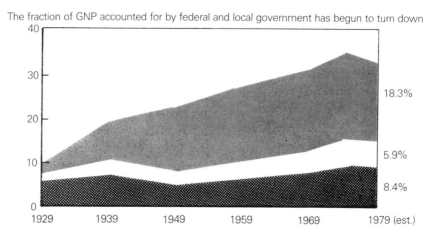

The fraction of GNP accounted for by federal and local government has begun to turn down

The reduction of federal grants-in-aid to state and local governments (see Figure 7.2), and stiffening taxpayer resistance have had a major impact on state revenues. Between 1976 and 1979 the proportion of the American public favoring a reduction in governmental services jumped from 30 to 39 per cent.[2] Consequently, between 1977 and 1980, sixteen states reduced sales taxes, twenty-two states reduced income taxes and nine states indexed their income taxes to the Consumer Price Index (CPI), thereby effectively reducing rates of revenue growth.[3] In fact, when measured in terms of the dollar's purchasing power, beginning in the late 1970s many states experienced decreasing receipts.[4] In 1980, total state operating revenues, adjusted for inflation, were 1.1 per cent lower than the preceding year.[5] By 1982, the height of the recession, state budget deficits totaled $1.9 billion.[6]

Local government fared little better. As recently as 1974, municipal governments in the United States were increasing their annual spending at a rate which exceeded growth of GNP. However, by 1977, local spending increases had declined to less than two-thirds of GNP growth and were no longer keeping pace with inflation.[7]

Figure 7.2: Federal and state aid to local governments as a fraction of local revenues from own sources, 1948–1978

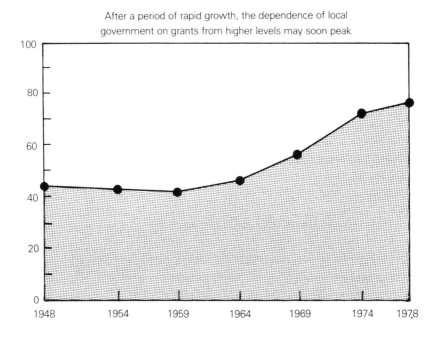

James W. Guthrie

American Education and the Economic Downturn

In general, education fared better than other government services during the 1976 to 1982 period of US economic instability. Although some states, such as California, did not protect education as well as the nation did on average, both higher and lower education services in the United States were better buffered from inflation and recession than were many other segments of the economy.[8] Higher and lower education revenues from all sources increased from $120 billion in 1976 to an estimated $197 billion in 1982, keeping education revenues even with inflation.

The Consumer Price Index climbed 61.2 per cent from 1976 to 1982. Education spending for kindergarten through twelfth-grade schools increased 62.4 per cent over the same period (Figure 7.3). In higher education, inflation adjusted per student spending increased 7 per cent from 1976 to 1981, from an estimated $6773 to $7263. Elementary and secondary class sizes also were reduced.[9]

Figure 7.3: United States Lower Education Spending Increases Relative to Consumer Price Index Changes 1976–1982

Year	CPI increase from prior year (%)	School spending increase from prior year (%)
1976	5.5	8.6
1977	6.6	6.8
1978	8.3	6.8
1979	12.1	9.2
1980	12.7	9.0
1981	11.0	12.2
1982	5.0	9.8
TOTAL	61.2	62.4

Source: 1984 Report of the President's Council of Economic Advisers and Inflation Measures for Schools and Colleges, Washington D.C., Research Associates of Washington, 1982.

Some states, local school districts, and higher education institutions did fare badly. Where extreme economic adversity coincided with enrollment decline, the outcome for schools and colleges was often traumatic. School and campus closures, shortened instructional days and years, bankruptcies, instructional supply shortages, salaries diluted by inflation, personnel layoffs, contractual defaults with vendors, and awesome backlogs of deferred maintenance occurred. Such burdens fell disproportionately on large city school districts — the ones frequently with students most in need of intense educational services, school districts in the northeastern region of the nation, and small, private liberal arts colleges. [10] Nationally, however, the education picture was less bleak. Why?

Political Decentralization, Revenue Diversity and Declining Demand

The answer to the above question resides in a combination of conditions. The decentralized manner in which US education is governed and operated, the diverse means by which education revenues are generated, and the dampened demographic demand for elementary-secondary education services occuring since 1971 acted in tandem to insulate American schools and colleges from the economic storm. A more complete explanation is in order.

Decentralized Governance

The United States federal constitution leaves primary responsibility for educational policy-making to state legislatures. Each of the states, with the exception of Hawaii, entrusts school operation to local districts. There are approximately 15,000 local school districts, and the overwhelming majority of them have elected boards of directors responsible for tailoring state policies to local preferences. In addition, there are thousands of non-public schools whose governance is generally outside of state legal provisions, and who serve approximately 11 per cent of the US grade school population and 22 per cent of total post-secondary enrollments.

The multitiered system for public schools is rendered even more complex by several social and political conditions which overlay governance. For example, at any particular education policy-making level, there exists a sizable cadre of significant political actors, for example, teacher unions, executive branch officials, and the judiciary. Additionally, public tastes for schooling vary by locality and region.[11] It is even possible to identify varying regional patterns of school governance resulting from historical development, economic conditions, and governmental structures.[12]

Higher education governance is substantially different but no less complex and decentralized. There exist approximately 3200 colleges and universities, including two-year colleges, almost equally divided between public and private institutions. The picture is confounded by the fact that a number of 'private' colleges and universities receive state and federal financial subsidies while 'public' institutions often are beneficiaries of large private financial donations. On balance, public institutions receive only 50 per cent of their revenues from local and state sources. Public colleges are usually governed by a board of regents or body of directors appointed by a state governor. Private institutions usually have self-perpetuating boards. These governing bodies may be influenced by federal government actions (for example, court decisions, research appropriations, and student aid programs), but as a group they possess sufficient authority and resources to adjust to all but the most prolonged and severe episodes of national economic distress, thus insulating them from adversity during periods of national economic instability.

If state or local officials for either higher or lower education, or public or private institutions, perceive that resources are falling below a level preferred by their constituents, within boundaries, they have the discretion to generate added revenues. However, their ability in this regard is mediated by consumer demand, state laws, and resource competition, which generally preclude rapid education funding increases. Also, if the national or regional economy sinks to a particularly low point, such as occurred in the Great Depression of the 1930s, state and local officials begin to see their discretion eroded by the absence of resources. However, though some regions have experienced sustained economic hardship, steep economic decline has not existed nationally for fifty years.

Diversity of Revenue

Decentralized decision-making in US education is accompanied by a multiplicity of revenue sources among levels of government. With few exceptions, local governments, both municipal and school, have exclusive access to property tax proceeds. State governments depend upon either sales tax receipts or proceeds from personal and corporate income taxes. A majority of states utilize a mix of these taxing mechanisms, but do not impose rates on incomes as high as does the federal government, which depends overwhelmingly for operating revenues upon a highly progressive personal income tax system.[13] To a much smaller extent, the federal government finances its operations from excise taxes and corporate income taxes.

Income and sales taxes possess substantial elasticity of yield, which means that receipts from these taxes grow or shrink at a faster rate than corresponding changes in income or sales.[14] The property tax is less elastic. It usually grows more slowly than income and sales tax revenues, in relation to increases in Gross National Product or Personal Income. However, the property tax is more resilient than these other taxes during economic downturns. When the economy is troubled, households may have less disposable income and may choose to reduce purchasing. However, they typically will pay taxes on their property as long as they reasonably are able.[15] The result is that locally generated school revenue is better protected than state and federal receipts during periods of national economic distress.

There exists widespread variation among states, but, nationwide, approximately 40 per cent of school spending stems from property tax revenues.[16] Even during the intense recession of the early 1980s, property tax revenues actually increased nationwide, giving school spending a measure of protection. States which depend less on property tax revenues for school support, for example, California, found themselves hardest pressed to sustain support for education.

United States higher education has a different but equally diverse pattern of revenue generation. Except for local subsidy of community colleges US higher education is funded by state revenues, private philanthropic contributions, endowment proceeds, and private user charges (i.e., tuition and student fees). Additionally, the federal government annually appropriates approximately $6 billion for student aid subsidies. Higher education is also supported directly by $.5 billion in federal funds and indirectly by approximately $15 billion in federal government research grants.[17] These latter monies assist students by supporting institutional overhead costs and providing school related employment for graduate students.

Because of heavier dependence upon state and federal revenues and limited access to property tax revenues, higher education institutions had to intensify their fund raising efforts and investment strategies in order to withstand the 1976–1983 period of economic distress.[18] They also raised tuition. Thus, though relying on a different set of resources than lower education, higher education institutions were still able to withstand the economic downturn. The exceptions were small, private, liberal arts colleges, heavily dependent upon tuition, and with little endowment upon which to rely.

However, since the beginning of the 1970s, institutions such as these have been in jeopardy also because of a shrinking age eligibility pool for admission and intensified competition from publicly supported colleges and universities whose fees are lower.[19]

Declining Demographic Demand

American lower education enrollments peaked in 1971 at 51 million students. By 1984, the number of pupils in public schools had declined to 40 million. Non-public school enrollments remained steady at approximately 5 million during this period. Northeastern states generally and large city districts of the east and midwest experienced the greatest drop in public school enrollments. The 'sun belt' states of the south and southwest experienced enrollment increases. Nationally, however, there has been a net decline.[20]

The consequences of enrollment decline have seldom been pleasant. School closures and teacher layoffs have occured in many local communities, despite vocal opposition of citizens and employees. However, an unanticipated consequence is that many school districts have become increasingly sophisticated regarding the management of decline. The period of inflation and subsequent recession was awkward, but for most school districts enrollment decline was only an incremental change in intensity, not a dramatic leap.

Higher education did not begin to experience a decline in its age eligible applicant pool until the mid 1970s. Even then, expansion in the percentage of high school seniors going to college and an increase in adults returning for post-secondary education buffered decline. Higher education is not expected to be intensely affected by demography until the early 1990s. Hence, it was only lower education which was insulated from the full shock of economic downturn by declining enrollment. The result was that there were fewer clients to serve and, thus, available financial resources did not have to be spread as far.

Economic Recovery

Beginning in the last quarter of 1982, the United States economy began to recover. By the middle of 1983, Gross National Product had surged to an annual growth rate in excess of 9 per cent and thereafter leveled off at a rate of 4 to 6 per cent that was predicted to be

Figure 7.4

The economic expansion leaves the torrid zone
(percentage change)

■ Real gross national product*

▦ Recessions

1980   1981   1982   1983   1984

*Seasonally adjusted annual rate.

Source: U.S. Department of Commerce, Chase forecast for 1981

sustained at least through early 1985 (Figure 7.4). At least until the last quarter of 1984, almost all other indicators of recovery were equally strong. Department of Commerce figures indicated that the manufacturing sector was at last beginning to tap its vastly underused capacity, plant utilization jumping from 67 per cent in 1981 to 81 per cent by the initial quarter of 1984. Unemployment had fallen from its December 1982 peak of 10.7 per cent to 7.1 per cent by the end of the second quarter of 1984. The dollar was climbing to its strongest point in history against other world currencies. There was the hope that this strong American economy would even fuel recovery for other nations.[21] Prospects for a favorable economic picture for industrial nations had not appeared better for a number of years.

... But, Uncertainty About the Short Run

Not far below the surface of current US economic optimism lurks a nagging doubt that the future is not altogether secure. There exists a strong element of uncertainty about the strength and lifespan of the recovery. In part this skepticism is triggered by lingering memories of the recent economic distress. Americans remain conscious of these conditions and continue to be fearful that they could be repeated.

Doubt is also provoked by federal government budget deficits, which in absolute dollar amounts are higher than at any time in the nation's history. Beginning with the 1980 fiscal year, and projected through 1989, the federal government spent and will spend substantially more than it has received and will receive in revenues (Figure 7.5). High budget deficits necessitate enormous federal government borrowing. Competition between private and public sectors for capital, combined with a fear of renewed inflation, acts to sustain high interest rates, discourage private borrowing and stunt economic expansion.[22] Industrial investment, housing starts and consumer purchases become threatened. Additionally, high interest rates sustain a strong dollar against foreign currencies, discourage export of US goods and services, and encourage imports. United States full employment is jeopardized as a consequence.

The solution to the problem of high interest rates is held to be a reduction in federal deficits. However, few political realists perceive that the deficits will be dampened sufficiently, regardless of the political party in office, to sustain economic recovery.[23]

Figure 7.5

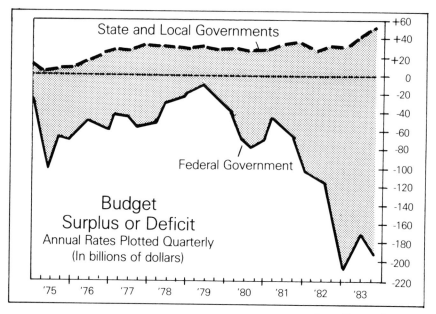

Source: Commerce Department

The Effect on Education

Short run uncertainty regarding the future of the American economy has had little effect upon contemporary education revenues or policies. Exceptions exist because economic recovery has not been uniform across regions or across industries. The general revenue picture, however, is brighter for both higher and lower education, at least for the short run. Most state and local governments have recovered from their mid-depression budget deficits and are now beginning to rebuild the capacity to spend for social purposes. Proposed budgets for public schools and state systems of higher education are higher in 1984 than at any time for the past four years. Public school teachers and college faculty will likely receive salary increases exceeding the rate of inflation for the first time in half a decade. However, long-term uncertainties regarding US economic productivity and competitive abilities have precipitated a forceful shift in education policy.

Longer run Economic Uncertainty and American Education Policy

Forces that shape public policy in the United States are generally too complicated to permit simple causal explanations. Nevertheless, one of the elements fueling the current drive to make education systems more rigorous and efficient is a deep concern for the nation's long-run economic health. For much of the twentieth century, the United States perceived itself to possess the world's most powerful economic engine. Americans enjoyed the highest standard of living. To be sure there were hard times, such as the Great Depression and world wars. Nevertheless, the United States had an economic system which produced benefits that could be more widely shared by its citizens than any other large industrialized nation. Although the American culture is ambivalent regarding intellectual matters, 'egg heads' and 'ivory tower' being widely used derogatory synonyms for intellectuals and schooling, it has been generally conceded that a powerful and open system of education, albeit necessarily aided by 'Yankee ingenuity', has fostered this productive economic climate.

This view of the world and the comfortable life that flowed from it began to be eroded in 1957 when the Soviet Union orbited *Sputnik*. Americans were surprised and shaken by his event. For the first time in a century, United States' technological supremacy was seriously challenged. The policy response was immediate. Education was held to be inefficient, devoid of rigorous standards, and insufficiently focused on math, science, and technology. In 1958 Congress enacted the National Defense Education Act, which provides states and local school districts with funds to buttress their instruction in scientific subjects and foreign language. Schools were challenged to assist in the recovery of American scientific and technological prowess.[24]

Events in the 1970s revealed that the United States and its economy suffered from more serious problems than simply Soviet space challenges. For example, throughout the 1970s, foreign car imports captured an increasing share of the American market, while Detroit, the symbolic hub of the American auto manufacturing industry, was reducing production, closing plants, and laying off workers.

What occurred for the automobile was to repeat itself in other important manufacturing sectors, such as electronics and steel production. American agriculture continued to be the production success story, and bioengineering was the big future hope. However, in the areas of greatest current economic growth, high technology electronics, magnetics, high temperature ceramics, lasers, precision metal casting, optics, and robotics, the United States was being challenged severely. Gross economic productivity measures had been declining since 1965 and now the practical consequences were becoming painfully evident.[25]

Beginning in the 1980s, an old link began to be reforged. An argument gained ground that there was an important connection between the unstable and sagging American economy and an ineffective American education system. While the United States produced lawyers, who contribute little by way of value added to the economy and international trade, Japan produced engineers. American industrial leaders complained that they could not recruit a workforce sufficiently literate to compete in high technology production with Germany, France and Japan. American labor was said to be overpaid and undereducated. If America is to compete effectively, then its schools had to be made more productive, more rigorous.[26] Harold Howe II, former US Commissioner of Education said: 'Frustration over the diminishing capacity of the US to compete in worldwide markets has awakened new interest in the old idea that the quality of human resources is a key element in the efficiency of the nation's economy'.[27]

The Eclipse of Equality

Public policy in the United States has been influenced strongly since the eighteenth century by societal concern for three major values, equality, liberty and efficiency. The three values are not consistently sought nor always accorded equal prominence. Public concern periodically will ascend on one value dimension and dilute popular attention to one or both of the others. Subsequent events may well rekindle interest in a submerged value and the sequence can repeat itself in a variety of combinations.

In the quarter century from 1955 until 1980, American education policy was dominated heavily by a concern for expanding equality.[28] Racial desegregation court decisions of 1954 initiated a twenty-five year span during which attention to issues of liberty (translated in education to concerns for greater schooling choices, greater curricula diversity, and more representativeness regarding school matters) were submerged by efforts to equalize or expand educational services for racial minorities[29], students from low income households[30], limited and non-English speaking students[31], students from low wealth and low spending school districts[32], handicapped students[33], and women[34]. Progress on these dimensions was not always consistent, and from time to time advocates of efficiency or liberty interests would emerge and forcefully gain control of the public agenda. However, policy momentum generally remained with those seeking to extend equality.

The 1980 election of President Ronald Reagan symbolized a turning point in American educational policy. His campaign opponent, former President Jimmy Carter, had attracted the electoral support of conventional advocates of expanded educational equality. Reagan, consequently, had an added degree of political discretion to heed the pent-up efficiency and liberty preferences of those who believed that American education had sacrificed academic standards in a drive to expand equality.

Liberty proponents were to be disappointed. The newly elected President espoused vouchers and tuition tax credits, but was never willing to mobilize and expend political resources to attempt their enactment. However, efficiency proposals were attractive to the Reagan administration. During his initial year in office, 1981, the President proposed and gained congressional approval for consolidating twenty-eight federal education programs into a single block grant, funds for which were ceded to the discretion of local and state education authorities.[35] The President's budget also held federal education spending stable. At least for a time, concern for equality was to be eclipsed by efficiency.

The Ascendance of Efficiency

Added national attention to educational efficiency is not a product simply of partisan presidential politics. Americans have been conscious of a fifteen-year decline in national average scores on Scholastic Aptitude Tests, examinations taken by high school seniors applying to college. Public opinion surveys repeatedly have reported that citizens believe school discipline to be lax. Studies reported that teenagers watch television more hours than they attend school. Anecdotes frequently appeared regarding the dismal state of literacy among America's workforce. These conditions were of a long standing nature. Why was it not until the early 1980s that their existence began to be considered seriously as a stimulus to education reform? There are at least three answers to this question.

International Economic Competition

A major answer is that it was not until the 1980s that there existed widespread public concern that an uncertain American economic future needed to be buttressed by a more productive system of education. America's academic decline was accompanied, though perhaps not causally, by the declining economic conditions already described. Upon closer examination, it became evident that not only did many of the competitor nations produce more effectively economically, but also they had more effective systems of education. Japanese students went to school longer and studied harder. French students were subjected to greater rigor. Soviet students absorbed more mathematics. It was now the likely case that schooling could make a difference for pupils and for a nation, and if United States' schools had fallen into a productive torpor compared with other nations, then, perhaps, school reform was in order.

Schools can Contribute to Academic Performance

For much of the 1960s and 1970s, while the academic performance of America's students was declining, the dominant popular interpretation of social science research was that schooling was a weak 'treatment' and had little chance of overcoming childrens' social and economic disadvantage. This view gained widespread attention with publication of the 1966 'Coleman Report'.[36] Subsequent efforts by methodological critics to dilute the negative policy impact of the Coleman Report had nowhere near the widespread currency of the original report conclusions.[37] Subsequent publications by individuals such as Christopher Jencks only solidified the view among policy makers and informed members of the public that schools were insufficiently powerful engines for achieving societal purposes.[38] It was during this period that proposals for bypassing public schools, for example, voucher plans, were widely publicized. Given the extensive perspective that schools made minor difference, it is little wonder that policy makers paid little heed to reforming them. This was particularly the case if the reforms held the prospect of absorbing additional sums of public money.[39]

By the latter portion of the 1970s, the research pendulum began to swing in the opposite direction. Improved social science predictive models and research techniques began to uncover school effects that were absent from the initial studies of the 1960s and 1970s.[40] Also, a study of school effects in England demonstrating the positive consequences of good schools drew substantial attention in the United States.[41] Similarly, studies conducted by World Bank economists in developing nations began to restore the view that schooling could make a difference in the academic performance of students.[42] If this was so, then reforming education was now more captivating as a public policy option.

Politics: A Catalytic Converter

Ronald Reagan's Presidential pronouncements were highly visible symbols of renewed attention to efficiency issues in education. However, the analytic foundation for the reform movement was laid substantially in advance of his coming to office. For example, several philanthropic foundations had previously funded studies of American schooling which were national in scope. In the 1970s, the National Institute of Education had sponsored research studies on school performance that were to serve in 1983 as the base for a highly publicized national report. What President Reagan did was recognize the intense political salience of education for American voters and begin to capitalize upon it. By 1984, his electoral campaign opponents from the Democratic Party had little choice but to try and outdo him in their announced desire for educational improvement.

Reagan's Secretary of the US Department of Education, Terrell Bell, had formed a National Commission on Educational Excellence, chaired by David P. Gardner, early in his term. The release of the Commission's report in 1983 was effective in gaining widespread attention from the American mass media. At this point, President Reagan took credit for the Commission and its report and began to publicize it even more intensely.

The report distilled numerous criticisms of American schools and pronounced several reform dimensions, for example, more rigorous secondary school curricula, better trained and better paid teachers, more homework and better textbooks, but the report makes little effort to analyze causes of school ineffectiveness. The assumption was that whatever the causes, recommended actions will suffice to cure them.

Had there been but one such report, perhaps it would have triggered intense but short-lived attention. However, the National Commission's effort was soon to be followed by other national studies, most reaching similar conclusions. American schools were insufficiently rigorous and higher standards of academic performance should be expected of them and their pupils.[43] The number of reports, the widespread base of their support in foundations and the business community, and the similarity of their recommendations rendered them difficult to ignore. These reports, and the popular pronouncements of the President and other visible political officials triggered intense but short-lived attention. However, the National skeptics and those who counseled caution.[44] On balance, however, the United States was embarking on one of the most intense efforts at educational reform in its history[45], and the major motive was to improve economic productivity.

Conclusion

Will the new reforms be effective? How long will the effect last? Who will benefit and who will suffer? Will it restore productivity to the economy and render America more competitive internationally? All these questions remain to be answered. Nevertheless, a shift has been made, and the United States is now pursuing greater productivity from its schools. This movement results only in small measure from recent experience with reduced resources. It is provoked to a far greater extent by a national concern that the nation's long run economic future hinges on building a more effective system of education.

Acknowledgements

The author wishes to express his appreciation to Guy Benveniste, Walter I Garms, David Lost, Richard Pratt, Philip Makan, Rodney Reed and Davis S Stern for useful comment on earlier drafts of this chapter.

Notes

1 Based on data from the President's Council of Economic Advisers and the Bureau of Labor Statistics in the U.S. Department of Commerce.
2 ADVISORY COMMISSION ON INTERGOVERNMENTAL RELATIONS, (1981) *Changing Public Attitudes on Government and Taxes*, Washington D.C., ACIR, p. 12.
3 EDUCATION COMMISSION OF THE STATES, (1982) *A Changing Federalism: The Conditions of the States*, Denver, ECS, p. 3.
4 *Time*, 28 November 1983, p. 27.
5 EDUCATION COMMISSION OF THE STATES, (1982) *op. cit.*
6 *Time, op. cit.*
7 ADVISORY COMMISSION ON INTERGOVERNMENTAL RELATIONS, (1979) *State-Local Finances in Recession and Inflation*, Washington, ACIR, p. 9.
8 An exceptional case is described by CATTERAL, J.S. and BRIZENDINE, E. (1984) *Proposition 13: Effects on High School Curriculum, 1979–83*, Program Report No. 84 B5, Institute for Research on Education Finance and Governance, School of Education, Stanford University, May.
9 Figures derived from *Conditions of Education* (1976 and 1983 edns) Washington D.C., National Center for Educational Statistics.
10 See CRONIN, J.M., (1981) 'Big city school bankruptcy', paper prepared for the Institute for Research on Finance and Governance of Education, Stanford University.
11 GLEN, N.D. and SIMMONS, J.L., (1967) 'Are regional cultural differences diminishing?' *Public Opinion Quarterly*, 31, pp. 176–93; and DOWNEY, L.W., (1960) *The Task of Public Education*, Chicago, Midwest Adminstration Center, University of Chicago.
12 WIRT, F.M. and KIRST, M.W., (1982) *Schools in Conflict: The Politics of Education*, Berkeley, Ca, McCutchan, chapter 4.
13 Social Security payments are made to retired and other eligible individuals from taxes levied on personal income matched by employer contributions. This is in addition to the federal personal income tax.
14 See GARMS, W.I., GUTHRIE, J.W. and PIERCE, L.C. (1978) *School*

Finance: The Economics and Politics of Education, Englewood Cliffs, N.J. Prentice Hall, chapter 6 for a discussion of tax elasticity.

15 In 1982, with the overall economy only beginning to recover, property tax receipts nationwide increased an astounding 13.7 per cent, the largest increase in fifty years, KIRST, M.W., (1984) 'State policy in an era of transition', *Education and Urban Society*, 16, 2, February, p. 229.

16 'Finances of Public School Systems, 1982 Census of Governments', 4, 1, Washington D.C., US Government Printing Office.

17 Federal financial figures taken from the *1984 Report of the President's Council of Economic Advisers*, Washington D.C., US Government Printing Office.

18 'Taking Risk with Endowment', *Wall Street Journal* 15 December 1983, p. 1.

19 Between 1976 and 1981, twenty-eight private four-year colleges closed contrasted with one public four-year college, NCES (1983) *The Condition of Education*, p. 96.

20 BUTZ, W.P. et al, (1982) *Demographic Challenges in America's Future* Santa Monica, Ca, Rand Corporation.

21 Such was indeed the case. By February of 1984, economic performance indicators for the seven major non-communist industrialized nations were all substantially elevated over the prior twelve and six month periods. See 'Leading indicators climb for seven major nations', *Wall Street Journal*, 29 February 1984, p. 6.

22 This is the conventional view of the consequences of a high federal deficit. See 'The credit scramble', *The Economist*, 14 January 1984, p. 35. A minority position holds that it is fear of inflation which contributes overwhelmingly to sustained high rates for borrowing. This camp contends that the flow of capital to the US from overseas, the enormous retained earnings of American corporations, and growing state revenue surpluses can supply all the money needed to finance both the deficit and economic growth. See SHILLING, A.G., 'And business saving is compensating for deficits anyway', *Wall Street Journal*, 10 November 1983, editorial, p. 40.

23 The public is concerned about the deficits. In a 1984 California poll, 78 per cent of respondents believed the federal government should do all it can do to reduce the deficit. In 1982, the comparable figure was only 60 per cent. *California Opinion Index*. Volume 2, February 1984.

24 Matters were perceived as being so dismal that a famous physicist of the day, GEORGE R. PRICE, was quoted in the 18 November 1957 issue of *Life* as saying, 'Few predictions seem more certain than this: Russia is going to surpass us in mathematics and the social sciences. . . . In short, unless we depart utterly from our present behavior, it is reasonable to expect that by later than 1975 the United States will be a member of the Union of Soviet Socialist Republics.'

25 Between 1948 and 1965, annual gains in economic productivity averaged 3.2 per cent. Between 1965 and 1973 the comparable figure was 2.4 per cent. In the next five year span it dropped to 1.1 per cent. By 1979, productivity was slipping negatively.

26 This is the thesis of the book by BOTKIN, J., DIMANCESCU, D., and

STATA, R., (1984) *Global Stakes: The Future of High Technology in America*, New York: Penguin Books. Also, see REICH, R., (1983) *The Next American Frontier*, New York, Times Books.

27 Quoted in *Kappan*, June 1984, p.65.
28 See RAVITCH, D., (1983) *The Troubled Crusade: American Education 1945–1980*, New York, Basic Books.
29 *Brown v. Board of Education* 347 U.S. 483 (1954).
30 Public Law 89–10 The 1965 Elementary and Secondary Education Act.
31 *Lau v. Nichols* 414 U.S. 563 (1973).
32 *Serrano v. Priest* Cal. 3d 584 (1971).
33 Public Law 94–142 Education for All Handicapped Children Act.
34 Title IX of the 1972 Higher Education Amendments (20 U.S.C. 1981–86).
35 Chapter II of the 1981 Education Consolidation and Improvement Act, Public Law 97–35, USC 20, 3801.
36 COLEMAN, J.S. *et al.* (1966) *Equality of Educational Opportunity*, Washington D.C., U.S. Department of Health, Education, and Welfare, U.S. Government Printing Office.
37 GUTHRIE, J.W. *et al.* (1971) *Schools and Inequality*, Cambridge, Mass, MIT Press.
38 JENCKS, C., (1972) *Inequality: A Reassessment of Family and Schooling in America*, New York, Basic Books.
39 The deadening effect of the Coleman Report findings on educational policy and financial support for schools is traced by MADAUS, G.F., AIRASIAN, P.W. and KELLAGHAN, T. (1980) *School Effectiveness: A Reassessment of the Evidence*, New York, McGraw Hill.
40 See, for example, DREEBEN, R. and THOMAS, J.A., (1950) *The Analysis of Educational Productivity*, Cambridge, Ballinger.
41 RUTTER, M.R., *et al* (1950) *Fifteen Thousand Hours: Secondary Schools and Their Effects on Children*, Cambridge, Mass, Harvard University Press.
42 See, for example, SCHIEFELBEIN, E., FALLEN, J.P., and SEPULVEDA-STUARDO, M., (1983) *The Influence of School Resources in Chile: Their Effect on Educational Achievement and Occupational Attainment*, Washington D.C., World Bank, Staff Working Papers 350.
43 A summary and analysis of eight of these reports is provided by GRIESEMER, J.L. and BUTLER, C.F. (1983) *Education Under Study*, Chelmsford, Mass Northeast Region Exchange Inc.
44 See PETERSON, P.E. (1983) 'Did the Education Commissions say anything', *Brookings Review*, 2, 2, winter, pp. 3–11.
45 The reform was made even more attractive by virtue of the fact that, except for possibly teacher salaries, the changes needed to gain added academic rigor are not all that costly. See KIRST, M.W., (1984) 'A new school finance for a new era of fiscal restraint', and McDONNEL, L.M., (1984) 'School improvement and fiscal retrenchment: How to improve education when resources are declining', chapters 3 and 4 in ODDEN, A. and WEBB, L.D. (Eds) *School Finance and School Improvement: Linkages for the 1980's*, Fourth Annual Yearbook of the American Education Finance Association, Cambridge, Mass, Ballinger.

8   The United Kingdom, its Political Economy of Education

Hywel Thomas
University of Birmingham
England

Introduction

Changes in economy, demography and ideology have contributed to the low morale and fractured confidence characteristic of many within the education systems of the United Kingdom today. The same factors hold the 'promise' of a dismal future. On economy, the United Kingdom's own recession was deeper and longer than those of other major western economies. Even in the mid-1980s, as the economy approaches a cyclical peak of activity, unemployment continues to rise. What is the explanation for this unemployment and what is its significance for the education system? Certainly some part of the high levels of UK unemployment are explained by the international recession which followed the emphasis given by governments worldwide on the control of the inflation induced by the oil price rises beginning in 1973. However, there is widespread agreement that the nature of the economic policies of UK governments since 1976, which have given overwhelming priority to controlling inflation, have added considerably to the total level of domestic unemployment. Moreover, there is little doubt that UK unemployment would anyway have risen above 1973 levels because of the chronic relative uncompetitiveness of the UK's manufacturing base. This has been made worse by the discovery of the country's own oil reserves under the North Sea which has given sterling a quasi petro-currency status. This has kept the exchange rate well above levels appropriate to the relative competitiveness of the economy and added to unemployment. Thus, we see that much, but not all, of the

143

country's unemployment is explained by factors other than the international recession. This unemployment has had a considerable effect upon the education system. One reason for this is that the unemployed pay no taxes and reduce the scarce public revenue resources for which education must compete. A second reason is that welfare payments for the unemployed add to the demands upon those same public sector resources. Fortunately for education and other public sector activities the tax revenue from North Sea oil has to some degree compensated for the revenue and welfare payments implications of unemployment. However there are demographic and ideological reasons why this has not been sufficient to protect the education service.

Consider the demographic factor. Condemned to slow growth for at least the next five years[1], governments must still face the imperatives of welfare demands and these are represented principally by the needs of an ageing population. Their needs, and those of more than 3 million unemployed, are likely to be seen as more urgent than those of an education system in which numbers are falling. A logic of retrenchment is indicated for a maintained schools sector where numbers of pupils are expected to fall from 7.7 million in 1984 to 7.2 million in 1991.[2] The same logic has been extended, not without controversy, to higher education where student numbers may fall from 565,000 in 1984/85 to 489,000 by 1996/97.[3] The exception to this logic has been the growth in educational provision for the young unemployed. Governments have responded to this by financing training schemes all of which have an off-the-job element provided by the further education sector. However, it is significant that these training schemes have been controlled through the government department responsible for employment and not education. Understanding the significance of this brings us to the ideological pressures on the education system.

The potent combination of economy and demography would seem to be problem enough for the education system, but changes in ideology add to its beleaguered position. Whilst academic analysis questions the nature of the relationship between spending on formal education and economic growth[4], British governments remain committed to the positive nexus between education and economic growth. However, this nexus is now characterized by a specific formulation which is profoundly altered, emphasizing vocational and technical preparation oriented to the needs of the economy's industrial, manufacturing and commercial sectors at the expense, as necessary, of principles of liberal education. It is an ideological position which was gaining prominence before the international recession which acted as an accelerator in spreading its influence within government departments and amongst prominent policy-makers in the major political parties. The five-fold increase in youth unemployment between 1975 and 1982 appears to provide further evidence of the lack of preparedness of young people for the world of work. As it is an ideological perspective unacceptable to many professional educators, it follows that their relative autonomy must be challenged if the supporters of this curriculum-specific ideology are to secure the changes they desire.

The next section begins by describing and discussing recent changes to rules and resources, but also gives an account of some of the alterations to educational policy and practice which are taking place. The final part of the section is concerned with identifying the underlying processes which explain how the supporters of an investment-oriented ideology are able to secure their preferences of strengthening such an orientation in educational policies. The subsequent section gives further consideration to alterations to policies, but its main emphasis will be to examine their outcome effects. It will, in particular, concentrate on curriculum issues, although in the case of higher education all this is taken to mean are the changes in the distribution of students as between courses in arts, science and medicine. In each section examples will be given from compulsory education, further education and higher education. The chapter ends with a brief conclusion.

The Prism of National Qualities

Politico-Educational Institutions: Changing the Rules

Alterations to the constitutional relationships tell us something about changes in decisional processes within the government of education, but an examination of recent legislation ostensibly suggests a rather confused picture, removed from the remorseless shift towards more central government power perceived by some writers.[5] However, if we take as our assumption that the aim is to reduce the current level of professional control in the curriculum, this confusion is clarified: professional control can be reduced by a combination of pressures from central government, local education authorities (LEAs) and the local community through governing bodies. The Education Act of

1979 returned to local education authorities the power to decide whether or not they wished to reorganize their secondary schools into non-selective comprehensive systems. The 1980 Education Act removed the obligation upon LEAs to provide school meals for all children, sought to strengthen community representation and authority on school governing bodies and increased the rights of parents to obtain for their child the school place of their choice. A 1984 Green Paper[6] suggests a further increase in the powers of governing bodies which would also have a parent majority, an unwelcome proposal to the LEAs. The 1984 Education Act has also been strongly opposed by local government associations because it earmarks for the Department of Education and Science (DES) a maximum of 0.5 per cent (about £35m in 1985/86) of the education element of the grant made by central to local government. Its purpose is '. . . to help innovation and to meet identified and agreed national needs'. The Labour Opposition in Parliament did not oppose the Bill. For the universities legislative intervention is proposed, to weaken tenure clauses for academic staff, enabling redundancies to be declared on grounds of financial stringency.[7]

Outside the area directly related to education legislation, there is stronger evidence of centralizing policies, particularly in relation to control of resources. The 1980 Local Government and Planning Act gave central government a mechanism to limit grant payments to local authorities deemed to be spending above the 'needs' level set by the central Department of the Environment. The 1984 Rates Act gives the same Department the power to limit the local taxation (rates) increases of local authorities. These two laws provide controls on spending levels but not its distribution, and it is the use within education to which the resources are put which concerns those who support an investment oriented curriculum. The annual 0.5 per cent from the 1984 Education Act is hardly likely to be a major factor in securing such a substantial change. We must look beyond legislative change.

There is an obvious distinction between possessing the legal means to do something and actually exercising that power. The DES has chosen to exercise such power more readily; for example, 'discovering' an entitlement in the 1962 Education Act allowing it to directly finance some in-service training.[8] Existing statutory powers have been used so that the Schools Council, believed to be overly influenced by teachers, has been abolished[9] and replaced by a School Curriculum Development Committee and a Secondary Examinations Council, appointments to which the Secretary of State for Education has firmer control. In 1981 the DES created an advisory body on non-university higher education, giving it much greater influence on institutions most of which are owned by local authorities.[10] The DES has also interpreted more vigorously its statutory responsibilities '... to promote the education of the people of England and Wales ... and to secure the effective execution by local authorities ... of the national policy ...'[11] It has, for example, produced a series of documents on the school curriculum designed to shape opinion in an area where government fiat would be viewed as unacceptable. The processes by which opinion is shaped and policy preferences secured will be considered further in the last part of this section. Before that, it is necessary to examine the impact of changes in resources and their influence on decisions and programmes.

Economic Resources

There has only been one major area of educational provision, in the United Kingdom, which has enjoyed substantial growth in recent years, and it has not been under the direct control of the DES or the LEAs; it is the Manpower Services Commission (MSC) of the Department of Employment (DE). Its most substantial responsibility is the Youth Training Scheme (YTS) introduced in September 1983. Through YTS, 16 year-olds, whether employed or unemployed, unemployed 17 year-old leavers in their first post-school year and unemployed disabled 21 year-old leavers, are financed for one year of training, largely employer based (71 per cent of places taken by trainees).[12] This training activity impacts principally on the further education (FE) sector, which caters mainly for 16 to 19 year-olds, because the MSC buys-in a minimum 13-week off-the-job element for its one-year scheme. This accounts for some 11 per cent (£90m in 1984/85) of funding of work-related non-advanced further education. Reflecting the government's confidence in the efficacy of MSC activity, it is planned to increase to 22 per cent (£200m in 1986/87) the share of this funding controlled by the MSC.[12] It is money which will be taken from the central government grant to local authorities and so reduces their discretion on spending. The same agency is also funding a Technical and Vocational Education Initiative (TVEI) for 14 to 18 year-olds in schools designed 'to open a technical and vocational route to recognized national qualifications'.[14] By September 1984 sixty LEAs (out of 103 in England and Wales) had these schemes, which must operate within a maximum budget for each LEA of

£400,000 per annum (£24m overall). The amount of MSC money funding these educational institutions (£114m, summing the FE and schools element in 1984/85) is only 1.2 per cent of the £9,300m budget for 1984/85[15] and bears no relation to the effect of the MSC on the education system. The explanation for this lies only in part with the fact that it is bringing new resources and change into a contracting system. Also significant is that as an approach to the curriculum it is in tune with the ideological emphasis of the central government generally and of many in the DES. This issue links to the processes of policy change but, before developing that theme, it is appropriate to complete the description of the resource circumstances of other sectors.

The total numbers of teachers employed by LEAs in January 1983 was 443,000, a figure which is expected to fall to 384,000 by 1991.[16] This contraction in total numbers masks a tendency for the pupil-teacher ratio (18:1 in January 1984) to improve because the LEAs have not reduced teacher numbers as quickly as the DES hoped. There have also been delays in reducing the number of school places in line with the fall in pupil numbers. This fall in numbers has caused several LEAs to reorganize the structure of secondary school-ing and create junior colleges for 16 to 18 year-olds. The proportion of resources spent on educational books and equipment has fallen, from around 5 per cent in 1975 to less than 4 per cent of school budgets by 1984, reflecting its position as a soft target for cuts, since it does not attract the same interests in its defence as teacher employ-ment levels or school closures.[17] The improvements in the pupil teacher ratio and increasing space have done nothing to abate the widely recognized fall in the morale of teachers in schools. Moreover, the management of contraction is altering important quantitative and qualitative characteristics of the teaching force which are occuring as an unplanned consequence of the most convenient way of managing numbers.[18] These last factors of quantity and quality exist also in the further and higher education systems, and may have important consequences for the quality of work in those institutions.

The changing budgetary relationship of the MSC with further education has been described and the uncertainty for teaching staff introduced by altering funding sources can be conjectured. In the case of higher education the possible reduction in student numbers has been described above and, for the universities in particular, this would add to the 10 per cent contraction in real terms they have undergone since 1981. It is significant that the general guidance to the universities from the University Grants Commission (UGC) in 1981[19] on the distribution of these cuts proposed a greater than average cut in arts, allowing for growth in areas more closely allied to the needs of industry and reflecting again the ideological question identified earlier. It is clearly time to consider the issues of values decision processes underpinning the changes in rules and resources which have been described.

National Values: From Consumption to Investment?

Implicit in this account so far is a belief in the existence of causal relationships which mean that alterations in rules of procedure and the distribution of resources do not just happen. Rather, either they occur because of shifts in the value positions and/or needs of powerful interests, or they arise from changes in the relative power of interests with conflicting values. It is a supposition of this chapter that the demands for an investment oriented curriculum and the challenge to professional autonomy arise because of the crisis of the UK economy, exacerbated by the world recession, and the belief of powerful interests that an education system more responsive to industrial needs will contribute to resolving the economy's problems. The purpose of this section is to explore the mechanisms and relationships which tend to work in support of the policy preferences of powerful interests in a liberal-capitalist economy. However, before beginning the analysis, it is worth emphasizing the considerable doubt which exists about the link between the cognitive skills and knowledge used at work compared with those transmitted in schooling. This *preparation* function is challenged by more compelling arguments about the *socialization* and *selection* functions of schools. It may be, therefore, that the pursuit of a more vocational curriculum as a means of improving the 'fit' between education and the economy is a chimera, the real investment function of education being its process of socializing individuals into their appropriate occupational categories.[20] Be that as it may, how do the preferences of powerful interests, whatever they may be, gain pre-eminence?

Several recent studies of central-local relationships in education in England and Wales[21] have used explicit theoretical models in their analyses, and some have recognized the problems of linking models (such as resource dependency theory) which identify actors behaving in a way '. . . close to our experience'[22] to those (such as neo-systems theory) where the '. . . framework is bereft of actors whose purposive agency would make sense of contradictions and conflicts'.[23] In his

Figure 8.1   An overview of the education system in England and Wales

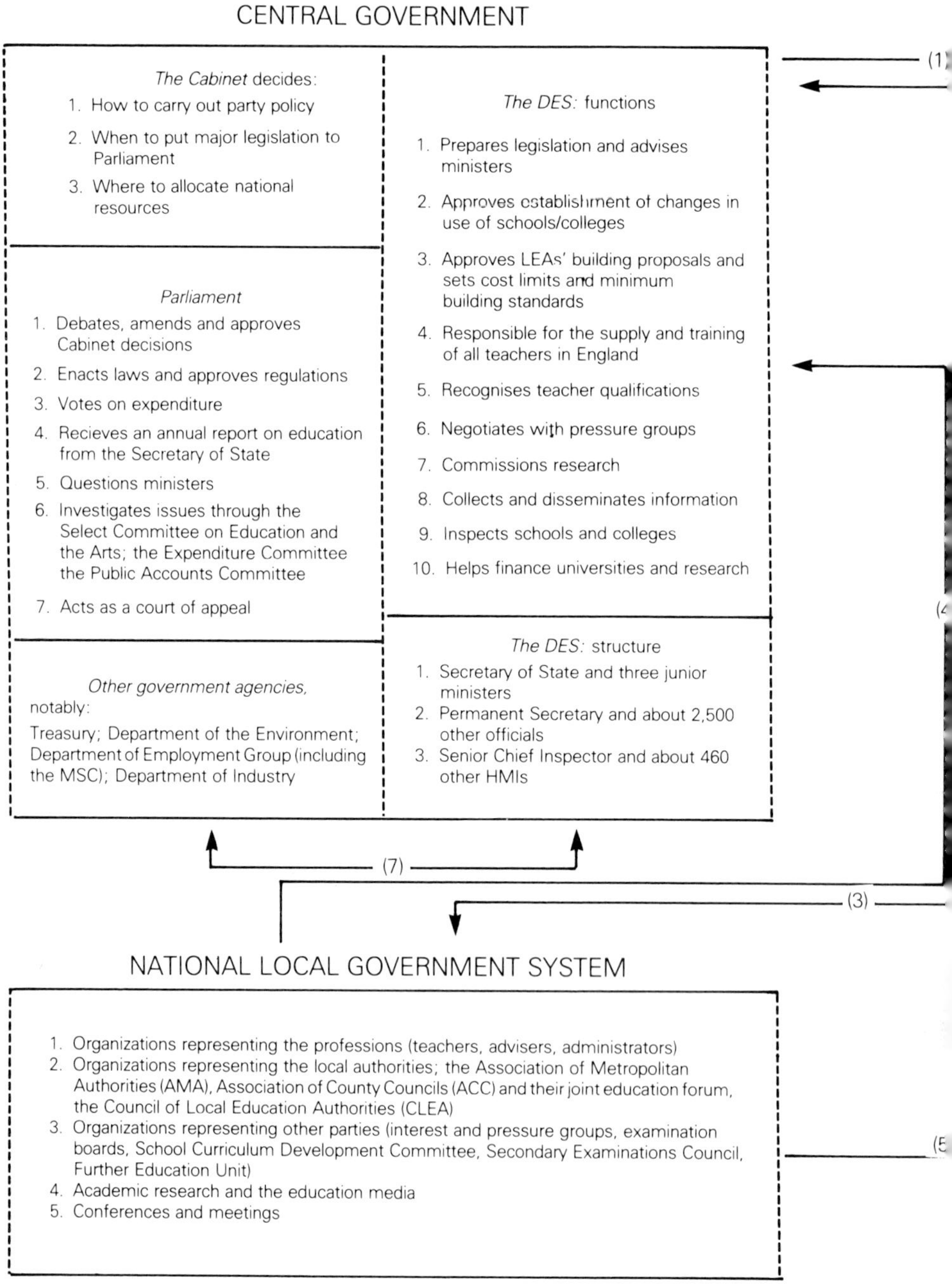

CENTRAL GOVERNMENT

_____ (1)

The Cabinet decides:

1. How to carry out party policy

2. When to put major legislation to Parliament

3. Where to allocate national resources

The DES: functions

1. Prepares legislation and advises ministers

2. Approves establishment of changes in use of schools/colleges

3. Approves LEAs' building proposals and sets cost limits and minimum building standards

Parliament

1. Debates, amends and approves Cabinet decisions

2. Enacts laws and approves regulations

3. Votes on expenditure

4. Recieves an annual report on education from the Secretary of State

5. Questions ministers

6. Investigates issues through the Select Committee on Education and the Arts; the Expenditure Committee the Public Accounts Committee

7. Acts as a court of appeal

4. Responsible for the supply and training of all teachers in England

5. Recognises teacher qualifications

6. Negotiates with pressure groups

7. Commissions research

8. Collects and disseminates information

9. Inspects schools and colleges

10. Helps finance universities and research

(4

Other government agencies,
notably:
Treasury; Department of the Environment; Department of Employment Group (including the MSC); Department of Industry

The DES: structure

1. Secretary of State and three junior ministers

2. Permanent Secretary and about 2,500 other officials

3. Senior Chief Inspector and about 460 other HMIs

(7)

(3)

NATIONAL LOCAL GOVERNMENT SYSTEM

1. Organizations representing the professions (teachers, advisers, administrators)

2. Organizations representing the local authorities; the Association of Metropolitan Authorities (AMA), Association of County Councils (ACC) and their joint education forum, the Council of Local Education Authorities (CLEA)

3. Organizations representing other parties (interest and pressure groups, examination boards, School Curriculum Development Committee, Secondary Examinations Council, Further Education Unit)

4. Academic research and the education media

5. Conferences and meetings

(5

Source: Slater, D. (forthcoming) 'The education sub-government structure and context', in Hughes, M.G., Ribbins P., and Thomas, H. (Eds.) *Managir Education: The System and the Institution*, Holt, Rinehart.

The DES does *not:* 1. provide or administer schools or colleges
2. determine the detailed curriculum of schools or colleges
3. choose or publish textbooks or teaching aids
4. set or mark examinations
5. pay or employ teachers

— (2) —

LOCAL GOVERNMENT

LEA: functions	Institutions maintained or supported by an LEA
1. Secures provision of schools and colleges 2. Builds, owns and maintains state schools and colleges 3. Appoints Governing bodies to be responsible for the general direction of state schools and colleges 4. Recruits and pays teachers on agreed national scales 5. Provides support services (e.g. school meals, school meals, school transport, careers and Inspectors/Advisers)	S C H O O L S *State maintained schools:* built and wholly maintained by the LEA *Voluntary controlled schools:* two thirds of governors represent the LEA which bears all the costs *Voluntary aided schools:* two thirds of governors represent the voluntary interest or foundation; the LEA bears certain costs e.g. teachers' salaries, maintenance and running costs *Special agreement schools:* about two thirds of the governors represent the voluntary interests; the LEA shares some of the costs *HEADTEACHERS* are responsible for the Internal organization, management and discipline in schools
LEA: structure 1. An education committee of elected and co-opted members of the local authority 2. A Chief Education Officer heading a team of officers and Inspectors/Advisers	C O L L E G E S *Governing bodies:* less than half the governors represent the LEA; the rest represent other local interests e.g. commerce and industry *Academic Boards:* unlike schools, colleges must have an academic board or other suitable consultative arrangement; this board has decision making powers in colleges with a substantial amount of advanced work, advisory powers in others *PRINCIPALS* are responsible for the internal organisation, management and discipline in colleges.

OTHER LEAS

(6)

LEAs do *not:* 1. impose curriculum, syllabi, methods or teaching materials on schools or colleges
2. set or mark examinations

influential book on urban politics Dunleavy[24] confronts this dilemma and develops a complex model which attempts to take account of structural influences and complex networks of interdependence and influence.

For the purpose of this chapter, it is useful to begin with his notion of inter-governmental flows of influence. Figure 8.1 shows a variant of this devised by Slater[25] for the education system of England and Wales and is included as a useful descriptive device.

Unfortunately, unlike Dunleavy's more abstracted chart[26], it does not show quasi-governmental agencies (QUAGOS) and their influence flows as a separate category; yet, these have grown rapidly in number, normally receiving powers previously vested in local authorities.[27]. The growth of QUAGOS, in addition to the growth of the scale of local government activity, contributes to '. . . a unique structure of "non-executant central government" . . .' (p. 103). Whilst the DES is an excellent example of a largely non-executant department it says little about its influence on determining education policy. This influence is indicated through '. . . the complex web of inter- and supra-authority relations' (p. 105) described as the national local government system. It is a reminder that individual 'local authorities do not make decisions about most aspects of policy in isolation' (p. 105) and, particularly, 'At an *ideological level*, the system provides an important source of values and ideas for actors in particular localties' (p. 106) and may play a key role '. . . in structuring, generalizing and accelerating processes of policy innova-tion in urban policy formation . . .' (p. 106).[28]

Within this complex of inter- and intra-governmental flows professionals in urban public services have a crucial role in channell-ing influence '. . . because the publicly-employed occupational com-munity normally interpenetrates central and local government'. An example of this is Her Majesty's Inspectorate (HMI) who may have been the critical agency legitimizing an ideology emphasizing a compulsory core to the secondary curriculum. As to their role in the debate on vocationalism, the known hostility of the previous Senior Chief HMI to TVEI must be set against the HMI-led innovative work of the FE Curriculum Unit (FEU) whose output has given an attractive format, rooted in the affective domain, to a 'new' vocational curriculum.[29] Local government education officers are another im-portant professional community in these relationships. In addition to being open to influence from the senior education professionals (HMI) their position makes them particularly sensitive to the choices enforced by resource limits. Thus a compulsory curriculum is likely to appeal because it is normally cheaper than existing models, and the TVEI initiative is seen as attractive because it brings new money into schools. This extra money also explains the positive response of schools to the scheme. In addition, because it is an innovation at a time of retrenchment, it may well attract the active support of able, ambitious and enthusiastic staff. If these produce a successful programme, which is quite likely given these factors and the extra resources attending the project, the case for extending this approach to the curriculum will be hard to resist.

The corporate economy is a third important influence on urban politics described by Dunleavy.[30] Its influence on education is considerably under-researched. However, Dunleavy's analysis of the role of large construction firms in public housing, 'big hospital' technology and motorway building might well be applied to the school building programme of the late 1950s and early 1960s.

> ... in seeking to define a public services market insulated from competition by smaller firms with lower overheads, the large corporations have at different times and in different services exerted pressure to increase the unit size of investment and to stress technological sophistication in construction solutions. (p. 122)

The regularity of the involvement of local authority Directors of Finance and their senior staff with the money markets is identified as an activity with an ideological effect, '... socializing key local authority decision-makers ... into the viewpoint and values of financial markets' (p. 126). The development of structures of corporate management, since the reforms introduced into local government outside London in 1974, will have brought senior education officers more closely into that web of influence.

Dunleavy does not explore the involvement of the corporate state in QUAGOS, but we should not ignore the influence networks between the corporate sector and government departments. These networks allow the 'needs of industry' to be represented, provide actors with a source of values and ideas, as well as a means by which joint policies can be devised. This network, acting as a source of values and ideas, may be the route of origin of the Audit Commission, which is in the process of producing so-called 'efficiency' check-lists designed to monitor expenditure patterns in local education expenditure. Whilst normally commissioning consultants from the corporate sector, their work is given legitimacy and expertise by adding a small number of local authority education officers to the teams.[31] In terms of joint policies, the National Economic Development Organisation (NEDO has representatives from government, employer organizations and trade unions) produced, in August 1984, a joint report with the MSC on training and education[32] which, among much else, challenges the acceptability of existing basic standards in schools and suggests a need to look at the existing pattern of 14 to 18 provision because it is not seen as producing an adequate flow of technically competent young people.

This analysis of non-local sources of policy change should not cause us to overlook local political influences as long as, Dunleavy warns, we do not play down how they are affected by 'broader social and economic influences' (p. 150). These manifest themselves through four significant influence networks: local party organizations, the 'burgher community', councillors involvement in local interest groups and corruption. The 'burgher community' is presented as '. . . the key unifying element or apex of what remains of local status systems', gaining coherence 'from the uniformly "middle class" bias of its membership . . . directly overlapping memberships between local government and other state agencies' which as '. . . a "community" also extends more widely through the social structure due to the prevalance of political nominations' onto the local judiciary, police authorities and the governing bodies of schools, the latter playing '. . . a considerable part in constituting local "educational opinion"' (p. 153). This part of the analysis allows us to discern the logic of the attempt to shift power to governing bodies via the 1980 Education Act and the 1984 proposals already mentioned. It is actually in step with other efforts to gain greater control of the curriculum. Governing bodies dominated by the 'burgher community' can be relied upon to add to the pressure on teachers to respond to the economic crisis by altering the orientation of the curriculum. Even the strengthening of parent representation can be seen as reliable, on the assumption that they will desire a greater instrumentality in the curriculum as a means of enhancing their children's employment prospects.

Through this complex web of relationships those supporting more liberal conceptions of education have lost ground, *in all sectors*, to those emphasizing the investment needs of the economy. It is a struggle which finds the former uncertain and lacking confidence about the role of education, whilst the latter believes it has some of the answers to the economy's chronic problems. However, they are likely to find, in the case of education, that it is easier to change policies than processes and outcomes.

Effects on Selected Policy Outcomes

The Compulsory Sector

In attempting to sensitize the school curriculum to the needs of industry the strategy adopted by a 'non-executant' DES has involved challenging the quality of performance of schools (i.e. the teachers) so that, in a chastened condition, teachers are more receptive to an alternative view of the curriculum. The capacity of teachers to resist is, concurrently, weakened by demography (falling rolls) and economy (declining teacher members) creating anxieties about future employment prospects. Beginning with the speech of the then Prime Minister, James Callaghan, in October 1976, there followed a flow of documents and initiatives on the curriculum,[33] some designed to maintain pressure on LEAs to monitor activities in schools, whilst others are general statements on content. The flow has altered the context of the debate and whereas, in 1976, a policy statement on content would have been seen as an unthinkable government fiat, such a major statement must now be seen as almost certain. Its power to influence schools will be reinforced by the change to a criterion-based examination system which will be introduced from September 1986.[34] However, how closely such a curriculum will fit the needs of industry is debatable for two principal reasons, the first of which is HMI and the second, the teachers.

Whilst prepared to criticize teachers for the performance of schools and their insensitivity to the 'world of work', HMI have also been prepared to lay responsibility for some failings on inadequate resources and, as described above, have also been hostile to a full-blown vocational curriculum.

In their own statements on the curriculum, as compared with those of the DES, there has been a greater emphasis on a liberal education. There is, nevertheless, a recognition of the need for relevance to the 'world of work' and, possibly as important, of the case for a compulsory core of subjects with a reduction in the proliferation of subject choices in the last two years of compulsory education. All other things being equal, a larger core is cheaper to service and is a useful legitimating argument for cuts.

The extent to which a work-relevant curriculum actually penetrates the classroom depends upon teachers. Whilst informal and some formal[35] evidence points to schools adjusting to such a view it is always sensible to be cautious about the extent to which classroom practice alters. Moreover, since teachers finally present and interpret material, their value judgments inevitably intrude and influence pupils' views of the work-relevant curriculum. Policies are not always transmitted into the outcomes expected or desired by policy-makers. This said, it is appropriate to take account of the earlier suggestion that, because of its embrace by enthusiasts, TVEI may be very successful. It is an useful example with which to end the section on schools because it reminds us, that if the DES fails to produce an adequately investment-oriented school curriculum, the MSC provides an alternative channel by which powerful interest can obtain their preferred curriculum policy. They are already well entrenched in FE.

Further Education

What is taking place in further education is, initially, a cause for some satisfaction but, fundamentally is a matter of profound concern. Although stimulated by the five-fold increase in unemployment amongst the under 18s between 1975 and 1982, the intervention by MSC can be welcomed in that it has made the first systematic and substantial effort to provide some education and training for the 300,000 or so school leavers with few or no educational qualifications.[36] Moreover, the problem has stimulated a review of the curriculum in this area by the FEU, whose

> ... concept of vocational preparation offered a new attempt to develop a curriculum of general education that is also not academic.... As such it has proved attractive to the MSC as it seems a way of producing a flexible work-force with process skills, such as planning and diagnostic skills, that can easily be transferred as the context of work changes in the economy.... Paradoxically, the expressive has now also become the instrumental: the notion of personal development has been transformed, through the medium of vocational preparation, into that of personal skills.[37]

So far so good, sound professional perspectives are influencing the 13-week off-the-job education element of YTS. But, '... the concept of vocational preparation is one of preparation for work' and, if 'real' work does not follow, what price the valuation attached by youngsters to the training scheme and its classroom element? Most obviously, it offers some challenge to the argument that education can prepare for work.[38] More disturbingly, by presenting personal skills material as part of a *vocational* education which has failed to deliver jobs, the legitimate merit of using personal skills material being used to improve the school curriculum will be much reduced, because it will be contaminated by a failed vocationalism. Once again we are reminded that policies can produce unexpected outcomes.

Higher Education

Cuts in the resourcing of higher education present an interesting case where it is possible to make tentative comparisons of the outcome effects of different systems of control. The cuts announced for the university system in June 1981 were fairly specific in their intended distribution as between different subjects areas. However, because the UGC does not have the power to direct how individual universities allocate resources, the informal evidence is of universities making savings wherever they might arise, which in practice means the rather unpredictable distribution of resignations as well as normal and early retirement. It has not followed that the universities have protected areas which accord with UGC and the DES' desires. More recently, in making resources available for the appointment of young academics ('new blood' posts) the DES and UGC have specified the areas of appointment, an active attempt at reducing the discretionary power of universities. By comparison, within the public sector of higher education, mostly institutions owned by LEAs and funded through central government grant, the creation of a National Advisory Body (NAB) has enabled the exercise of firmer direction and more detailed control on the distribution of courses and their unit costs. The case of teacher training represents a specific example of how systems of control can operate. It is also an hybrid because the Education Act of 1944 gives to the Secretary of State responsibility for course approval, whether it is based in a university or a public sector institution. This power has now been used to create a new accreditation body which must examine and approve all existing or new training courses, using criteria promulgated by the DES.[39] It is not surprising that courses must in future give attention to '. . . in particular, ways in which pupils can be helped to acquire an understanding of the values of a free society and its economic and other foundations'.[40]

In all sectors it would seem that much power and influence, whichever is appropriate or available, is being used to change the emphasis of the activity of institutions towards the investment needs of the economy.

Conclusion

It has been the purpose of this chapter to describe, explain and analyze how international and domestic economic factors, demography and ideology have affected the education system in the United Kingdom. Changes in economy and demography alone have contributed to important developments in policy, such as the closure of schools, the emphasis on a common core for the school curriculum, the creation of junior colleges for 16 to 18 year-olds, provision for the young unemployed and the cuts in numbers and resources in higher education. However, when we add the effect of ideological change, itself reinforced by the effects on the UK of the world recession, to economy and demography, it serves to considerably strengthen the investment orientation of policy for the all-important curriculum. But, because the direct controls upon the curriculum available to the executive seem comparatively weak, the chapter has drawn a distinction between changes in public policy and their actual effects upon educational practice and outcomes. This does not mean that those opposed to an investment-oriented curriculum should become too complacent because of the apparent weakness of these linkages. First, I have argued that the series of government documents on the school curriculum since 1976 has altered the view of the limits of government action in this area. Those limits are likely to continue to be altered, leading to increasingly specific policies on curriculum content. Second, I have suggested that the likelihood of TVEI being seen as a successful innovation must be very high, creating more pressures for its extension. Third, we have, with the example of the takeover by MSC of 22 per cent (so far?) of the non-advanced FE budget, evidence of the power of the 'investment interest'. Fourth, the mechanisms for controlling the distribution of resources in higher education are being altered, with significant consequences for the availability of particular courses in the future. Finally, since the problems of the economy are likely to continue, there is no reason to expect the economic and ideological pressures on the education system to relent. Nevertheless, although a demoralized and divided education system is no obvious match for the powerful interests who support these pressures, what are its prospects of mounting effective resistance?

In the case of higher education, we have seen that the prospect must be for a gradual alignment of course distribution and student numbers to the preferences of the DES. For the FE sector, control of a substantial proportion of its budget has already been moved to the MSC, which negotiates its preferred curriculum with its providing institutions. In the case of schools, the struggle over the curriculum is by no means resolved. In addition to the difficulty of penetrating teacher control of the classroom, we should not overlook the importance of the role of HMI in resisting an overly-specific prescribed curriculum which is also heavily investment-oriented. HMI are the leading professionals whose support is needed for legitimizing curriculum ideologies and, because some account must be taken of their values and ideas, a compromise may emerge where concessions are made in recognizing the importance of the 'world of work' and parts of the curriculum are specified as compulsory. Such changes would fall well short of vocationalizing the curriculum. They may provide teachers with sufficient confidence to resist the blandishments and pressures of the well-resourced and much more vocational TVEI project, and get on with the job of developing a vigorous and effective liberal curriculum appropriate to the complex needs of the next century. To HMI, then, may fall the task of preventing a depressed and decaying economy creating an education system in its own image.

Notes

1 BECKERMAN, W. (1979) 'Does slow growth matter? Egalitarianism versus humanitarism' in BECKERMAN, W. (Ed.) *Slow Growth in Britain: Causes and Consequences*, Oxford, Clarendon Press p. 2.

2 These figures are for England and Wales only, as are many of the examples and cases cited in this chapter. Scotland and Northern Ireland are separate sub-systems with several organizational differences from the English and Welsh systems. However, it is reasonable to take the analytical part of the chapter as applying to the whole of the United Kingdom. The figures on school population given here are from ACSET, (1981) *The Future of the Teacher Training System: Initial Advice to the Secretaries of State*, ACSET 81/24, London, DES, August.

3 DEPARTMENT OF EDUCATION AND SCIENCE (1984) *Report on Education No. 100*, 'Demand for higher education in Great Britain 1984–2000' London, DES, July.

4 BLAUG, M. (1983) *Where Are We Now in the Economics of Education?*, special professorial lecture, University of London Institute of Education.

5 See for example BECHER, T. and MACLURE, S. (1978) *The Politics of Curriculum Change*, London, Hutchinson; or LAWTON, D. (1980) *The Politics of the School Curriculum*, London, Routledge and Kegan Paul.

6 DEPARTMENT OF EDUCATION AND SCIENCE (1984) *Parental Influence at School: A New Framework for School Government in England and Wales*, Cmnd. 9242, London, HMSO.

7 See 'Will promotion mean loss of tenure?', *Education*, 164, 10, 7 September 1984, p. 186.

8 SLATER, D. (forthcoming) 'The education sub-government: Structure and context' in HUGHES, M.G., RIBBENS, P. and THOMAS, H. (Eds) *Managing Education: The System and the Institution*, Holt, Rinehart, chapter 2.

9 See PLASKOW, M. (Ed.) (1985) *Life and Death of the Schools Council*, Lewes, Falmer Press.

10 See 'New Chairman for curriculum committee' *Education* 162, 8, 19 August 1983, p. 138, 'Agreement in principle on two-tier central body', *Education* 158, 18, 30 October 1981, p. 332; 'NAB to become permanent says Sir Keith', *Education*, 164, 5, 3 August 1984, p. 84.

11 Education Act, 1944, section 1, clause 1.

12 'MSC release take-up figures for scheme', *Education*, 162, 26/27, 23/30 December 1983, p. 514.

13 Department of Employment/Department of Education and Science (1984) DE/DES, *Training for Jobs*, Cmnd. 9135, London, HMSO.

14 *Ibid.*

15 Budget figure calculated for the schools and non-advanced further education sector in England and Wales from (1984) *The Government's Expenditure Plans, 1984–85 to 1986–87*, Cmnd. 9143-II, London, HMSO.

16 Compiled from Cmnd. 9143-II and 'Teacher Numbers — looking ahead to 1995', *DES Report on Education*, No. 98 London, DES, 1983.

17 A fuller discussion of these issues is to be found in THOMAS, H., (forthcoming) 'Provision, process and performance in compulsory education: An economic perspective on changing enrolment' in HUGHES, M.G. *et al* (Eds) *op cit*.

18 *Ibid.*

19 UNIVERSITY GRANTS COMMITTEE (1981) Circular Letter, 10/81, London, UGC, 1981.

20 Useful but brief accounts of these issues can be found in BLAUG, M. (1983) *op. cit*; WATTS, A.G. (1983) *Education, Unemployment and the Future of Work*, Milton Keynes, Open University Press; and WILLIAMS, G. (1982) 'The economics of education: Current debates and prospects' *British Journal of Educational Studies*, Vol. XXX 1, February pp. 97–107.

21 As examples, interesting analyses are offered by RANSON, S. (1980) 'Changing relations between centre and locality in education' *Local Government Studies*, 66, November/December, pp. 3–23; and SALTER, B. and TAPPER, T. (1981) *Education, Politics and the State, The Theory and Practice of Educational Change*, London, Grant McIntyre.

22 RANSON, S. (1980) *op cit*, p. 17.

23 *Ibid*, p. 20.
24 DUNLEAVY, P. (1980) *Urban Political Analysis*, London, Macmillan.
25 SLATER, D. (forthcoming) *op cit*.
26 DUNLEAVY, P. (1980) *op cit*, p. 109.
27 *Ibid*, p. 103.
28 Dunleavy's generalizing and accelerator concepts have been developed and applied, in rather different ways, to the case of secondary school reorganization by PATTISON, M. (1980) 'Intergovernmental relations and the limitations of central control: Reconstructing the politics of comprehensive education' *Oxford Review of Education*, 61, pp.63–89; and RIBBINS, P. (forthcoming) 'Comprehensive secondary reorganization: A case of local authority policy-making?', in HUGHES, M.G. *et al* (Eds) *op cit*.
29 See SLATER, D. (forthcoming) 'Sixteen to nineteen: Towards a coherent policy?' in HUGHES, M.G. *et al* (Eds) *op cit* for a discussion of the 'affective' developments in the vocational curriculum.
30 DUNLEAVY, P. (1980) *op cit* pp. 120–30.
31 This occurred with their study of the non-teaching costs of secondary schools in 1983/84 and the study of teaching costs begun in 1984.
32 MSC/NEDO, (1984) *Competence and Competition*, London, NEDO.
33 In the eight years from October 1976 there have been over a dozen major documents on the curriculum, in whole or in part, published by the DES and HMI. The most recent discusses the organization, content and time allocation to subjects within the compulsory sector, from 5 to 16.
34 'GCSE: two into one will go' and 'Exams', *Education* 163, 26, 29 June 1984, p. 526 and pp. 522–3.
35 See WATTS, A.G. (1983) *op cit*, chapter 3.
36 SLATER, D. (forthcoming) *op cit*.
37 *Ibid*.
38 Evidently the labour market must have vacancies. It is a reminder of the argument that YTS may also need to be viewed as a social policy, '. . . of social order and social control' *Ibid*.
39 Department of Education and Science 'Initial teacher training: Approval of courses', *Circular No. 3/84* London, DES.
40 *Ibid* annex, para. 12.

9　The Editors: A View Across the Board: The International Recession and Educational Policy

Frederick M. Wirt
University of Illinois
USA

Grant Harman
University of New England
Armidale, Australia

A rich gamut of national experiences transpired during the period of international recession which our authors have explored. A new nation emerged on the world scene (Papua New Guinea), and another suddenly faced transfer to another world power (Hong Kong); a military coup replaced a civilian government in yet another (Nigeria); and China went through an amazing transformation in ideology and public policy that opened it to the world market. Democratic societies saw parties voted out and their opponents voted in. But our purpose in this chapter is to filter these diversities through the common concept of an international recession to determine effects upon these nations' economic resources, values, governance and polices of education, and some special issues. We will use each of these topics to summarize the experiences of our eight nations, and then derive conclusions about the relationship between the world village and national educational systems.

Effects Upon Economic Resources

The international recession hit our nations with effects ranging from great severity (most common) to indifference (China). Several patterns developed, but in all but one this recession had some important effects.

The Hard-Hit Nations

Particularly grim were the situations in Canada, Hong Kong, the United Kingdom (UK) and the United States (US). Here, large inflation and unemployment placed severe stress on government budgets, as well as creating havoc with personal lives. In all, public sector expenditures became fair game for businessmen and officials seeking to cope with these effects, and one sector to be influenced was education.

The inflation-unemployment figures reached staggering proportions in Canada and the UK, and even now they are well behind the recoveries that took place in two other hard-hit nations — Hong Kong and the US. In Canada, these economic consequences increased school leaving, while their teachers found themselves no longer 'sacred cows' in the struggle for government budgets. In the UK, the recession hit deeper and lasted longer than others. Its domestic economy suffered from much criticized problems — a premium on controlling inflation rather than unemployment (also an American emphasis during the Reagan administration), an over-valuation of its currency, and the absence of enough competitive manufacturing base. In both nations, the efforts of opposing party governments to deal with the issues were not successful, even when conservative parties were elected.

In the US, the recession plowed deeply, but its economy recovered enormously after the 1982 recession which had approached the depths of the 1930s depression. But before that recovery, inflation and unemployment hit 'double-digit' percentages. However, extensive energy conservation and oil import restrictions enabled the nation to mitigate effects of the oil boycott and its impact on 'petrodollars'. One national agency raised interest rates to record levels, which was probably the single factor most responsible for later controlling inflation. Trade unions accepted tighter wage and working agreements, and as a result productivity improved. Military spending helped stimulate the economy in some — but not a large — part, although as a result of it, that nation now faces an unprecedented deficit and national debt.

In Hong Kong, the worst recession known recently came amid crisis over return in 1997 of that former British colony to the People's

Republic of China (hereafter, China). This '1997 China Syndrome' found an economy of unparalleled growth which had given it a 'facade of prosperity'. However, an accompanying, massive immigration also generated demands for public services including education — which overwhelmed the government's budget. Real estate development — the basis of the late 1970s boom — collapsed through over-speculation. Exports to the US fell, thereby generating unemployment, the Hong Kong dollar fell — and amid all this the 1997 China Syndrome surfaced. The recession might have been ridden out, but this political issue interfaced with it to feed fears about the economy's future. By 1984, a mild rebound was under way, but government reserves were low and deficits were high.

The Moderate Effect Nations

Other nations were hit with somewhat less impact. Australia's strength in minerals and fuel oils helped fend off the severest effects of the international recession, Papua New Guinea's struggles to establish its new nationhood after 1975 were mixed with problems of world prices, and Nigeria's complications with military coups were compounded by the oil glut of the 1980s. In all these, no severe damage on these nations' economic resources is reported, but in all, some effect set back economic development.

In Australia, boom vs. bust periods, accompanied by Labor vs. conservative governments, had effects on education policy noted later. But compared with the hard-hit nations, this nation had valuable exports, a sound currency and capital investment funds not bound by high interest rates. Also, it had not been as dependent upon imported fuel oils as other industrial nations, so the petrodollar drag on the economy was not as heavy. Papua New Guinea (PNG), found the recession slowing its efforts to secure economic independence after 1975. While reducing Australian support of its own budget ('internal revenue'), it was still 27 per cent in 1983. The recession hit hardest because of PNG's reliance upon importing mineral fuels and lubricants (21 per cent of all imports in 1981). Conversely, PNG's export of its own minerals, as well as its fuel imports, put it at the mercy of world prices. Also, as noted later, it faced great internal divisions bubbling up through its devolved, federal system.

It is difficult to judge the full impact of the international recession upon Nigeria, because it both contributed to and was hurt by it. Its own finances were affected by that recession, because the oil glut slowed public spending for all services, including education. Neither a civilian nor two military governments could cope with these effects, particularly in trying to pay for construction of an expanded educational infrastructure. The situation worsened by 1982 when world oil demand fell off. Nigeria today is dependent upon imported goods, faced with an unstable price market abroad, and struggling with underfinanced national plans.

The Deviant Case

The world economy has had little impact upon China's economy, the single deviation from the serious effects noted elsewhere. The explanation lies in its ability to build buffers against the intrusion of unwanted effects and in the availability of resources to protect itself. While it is now opening to world trade, a part of the new move toward the concept of 'interdependence', it also managed to protect itself against recession, China did not have to rely upon high interest rates or high costs for fuel or other imports because — as the World Bank reported — it maintained a favorable balance of trade, huge reserves, a balanced budget, and a little commercial debt — programs dear to the hearts of conservative capitalists. Indeed, so secure was China that it helped its own economic advancement by lending billions of its reserves abroad (especially to Hong Kong). It was also insulated because it had a huge domestic market for most of its finished products and did not have the technology or capacity for foreign trade in more sophisticated products. However, China could become more vulnerable to market conditions abroad as it seeks to build up an export trade. Also, this expansionism constrained by ideological and political forces at home, cannot be regarded as permanent unless the current ruler's support for it is continued by his successors.

Conclusion

Despite the success of one nation — with large capital and other resources and with full political control of its economy — defence against waves that crash through the world village are extremely difficult. These results demonstrate the openness of the world village and its market where all villagers trade. But did this intruction upon national economies also generate effects upon the governance and policy of these nations' educational systems?

Effects Upon School Governance and Policy

In answering this query, the review of national response here found much greater variety in what happened than was the case for economic resources. It is as if the effects became diffused within the internal governance structures and between political parties contending over responses to the recession.

School Finance Responses

With economies constricting everywhere but in China, educational finances became one of many public services whose budgets could be cut. But these nations took four different strategies of response to recession. Some cut budgets, some maintained them, some even expanded them and one sought to redistribute them without cuts. And in the US, different regions used different strategies.

The cut strategy

In the UK, contraction pressures arose from the dire straits of the national economy. A common pattern under contraction was to fasten on education as fair game, particularly when teachers' 'militancy' had offended many traditional and conservative politicians. This attack took the form of asserting the influence of local and national elected officials over professional control. But these pressures also reduced the number and quality of teachers, the number of pupils, the funds for books and equipment, and so on. The vocational education pressure will be noted below.

In Canada, the national level of financing provincial education served to alter inter-level influence (noted later) under pressure of the recession. That pressure not only was followed by cuts in educational revenue but a decline in educators' status. The federal government's influence came through implementing a wide range of cost-cutting measures, such as teachers' salaries, and by reducing funds normally used to reduce inter-province spending differentials. This national effort had a 'steering effect' upon subsequent decisions made by provincial and local levels on their own budgets. Again, underlying all these shifts in moneys and decisions was the opportunity generated by an economy constricted by the international recession.

The Nigerian government funded education heavily under the military, and leaned greatly upon educational professionals for advice on allied schooling matters. But when the recession and its own falling oil markets appeared, educational spending dropped and national plans for schooling were cut back. While the civilian control under the 1979 constitution reversed military centralization and spawned party government, professional guidance was often ignored if it countered party goals. Especially troublesome were the grandiose plans for expanding this function without regard to the costs involved; indeed, this government ended up not paying for some school construction. The recession-caused 1982 austerity closed schools in two states and floated the possibility of parents paying for education. This dissatisfaction was one element leading to the second military government in late 1983.

In short, in nations using the cut strategy, there were no financial reserves and no political backing that would protect educational goals. Centralized or recentralized programs were a major response, accompanied by reduced schooling resources.

The differentiated cut strategy

It is possible that national policy currents may not have the same effect in every section of the nation. Strategies may be differentiated in terms of what the national government does or what the state-provincial reactions are. For example, recession caused the national government to adopt split educational programs in PNG. It resisted the recession-inspired contraction when it funded fully the program for primary education. However, the government yielded when it reduced support for secondary and higher education. Even in the worst year of the economy, 17–19 per cent of its national budget went for education. Of course, that goal was assisted by three loans from the World Bank. Consequently, despite its desire to devolve authority for education policy, PNG's national government has continued to wield great influence on its size and development. For example, the goals of universal primary education was part of its national plan, made possible by its own funding among the different states of PNG. Nationalizing influences continue, though. While the Education Act of 1983 made this function jointly managed by national and state levels, when 90 per cent of all school revenue originates with the national government, great power must follow in its wake. It is not surprising, then, that there was debate over limiting the states' authority under some circumstances.

Another differential reaction to the international recession occurred in the US, where regions were affected differently. In effect, the diversity of the state local-based education system could divert some national effects of the recession. However, the areas worst off economically (big cities and the northeast generally), suffered much more than the developing Southwest and most suburbs. Also, higher education and small, liberal arts, private colleges were harder hit than other levels and types of education. Overall, despite huge national deficits, the outlook remains bright for school finances. Meanwhile, tighter budgets caused a closer look at educational productivity, and the press gang of reformers are now sweeping the nation for recruits.

The key point here, though, is that the diversion and even muffling of recession effects were possible because of educational decentralization, revenue source diversity, and demographic slackening in schooling demands. Notice also that such diversion are possible when national involvement in this function is limited. It provided only 8 per cent of local school costs at its peak, and when regional economies vary in their strength and vulnerability to recession. These conditions are polar opposites of the case of PNG and Nigeria, where national control over the states grew.

The expand strategy

The world village thesis should not include nations which actually expand educational policies and finances under the crunch of this recession. But again, China resisted this intrusion, and Hong Kong less so.

In China, great changes were under way, traceable primarily to the domestic environment. A major program change was the rejection of the quick-fix solution for education, namely, a mass-based development program. Rather, from a desire to participate in the new technology, improved educational and managerial components of the labor force were required, which meant moving education higher up the priority list of national resources. Justification for such a shift required that recession be seen not as a part of the class structure or as consumption-oriented, but rather as a production force and hence a target for investment. These ideas, while issued from the top, faced political obstacles. Bureaucrats of other societal functions protected their own share of national resources, and decentralization to provinces and cities made difficult a national implementation of such policy. At heart, the issue was a division over spending money for primarily the best students or for comprehensive schooling, a top-down vs. a bottom-up strategy, familiar elsewhere.

In nearby Hong Kong, expansionist pressures for more education could not be resisted, as the migrant masses demanded education. Most schooling there is funded by the government but run privately through religious or other non-profit agencies. Response to the demand has been to provide enormous outlays for primary education, but the money for secondary or higher education fell off drastically. The interaction of the recession and the 1997 China Syndrome meant that reform of schooling was postponed, despite the recommendations of a prestigious panel of experts from other nations. The panel's views were accepted by the government, but only for the future, a future increasingly uncertain as 1997 approaches. Local control was instituted (which could casue later problems for China's control after 1997), and education was seen as part of the ' "stability and prosperity" survival kit' to meet the crisis. So, while the recession constrained schooling plans, this healthy economy at its worst was still growing at over 2 per cent, enough to expand schooling funds at least at the primary level.

But in both the cases of China and Hong Kong, the expand strategy required a healthy economy and national control of educational finance. Some expansion also took place in more prosperous regions of the US also, although national control did not exist.

The redistribution strategy

Besides a total cutback of expansion, one nation — Australia — sought to redistribute educational control and finances in the face of this international recession. Here, the mediating factor was the presence of parties with contrasting ideas about how national school funds should be managed. Labor governments in national and state levels had a more differentiated policy and favored public education more, spending according to differentiated needs among different students. The non-labor governments, on the other hand, tended to spend through per capita grants which put more into private schools. It also required 'streaming' different groups of students, developed more exams for those leaving schools, and turned more toward worker education programs (reviewed later). When Labor returned to power at the national level again in 1983, its new programs were widely redistributive but not expansionist (compared with the 1970s) and turned again to support public schools more. Even in a nation with little history of national control over education (although its funds much of it), the governments of that nation can redistribute their funding and programs, depending upon who is in power in Canberra.

Policy strategies and diffusion of influence

The potential effect of an international recession upon education was diffused by national differences in center vs. peripheral control, in economic conditions and so on. However, in all but China and Hong Kong, there were actual effects upon education strategies, whether cuts maintenance or expansion. The point here is not that the external influence had no effect, but its effects were differentiated by national institutions. Were it possible to question national leaders to ask if different policies would have been adopted in the absence of this recession, it is extremely likely they would report a more expansionist set of policies and funding as in pre-recession days.

Effects Upon Control

Another type of recession effects lies in answers to the question: Who governs? Repeatedly there were reports, both in federal and unitary systems, of shifting power relationships between the national and state-provincial-local levels of school governance. In no case was there a report of decentralization of the local level; rather, the terms regularly used are 'centralization' and 'recentralization'.

Within unitary systems

The results within unitary systems are best seen in the UK, where local professional autonomy was weakened by the challenge of local and national elected officials. Not only the professionals' power but also their emphasis upon liberal education were challenged. The opportunity for such challenges lay in a constricted economy where budget-cutting was imperative. That need raised questions about the relative utility of spending for discrete programs — all of which made it difficult for professional educators to demonstrate the importance of their ideas in the long-run. In political bargaining, long-run gains are usually ignored under the pressure of short-run advocates.

In China, the devolution of some budget decisions to the province level put education in competition with other functions, whose spokesmen could portray it as trivial or only a part of the superstructure, compared with their own productivity-enhancement programs. While the authority of the national leaders supported gearing up education to produce trained personnel needed for the new move into foreign trade and technology, that authority could not compel obedience among those other elements which saw national budgets as redistributive struggles over whose goals would be achieved. Provincialism remains strong in this education funding contest, one of the several evidences of the devolution of power from the single leaders that characterized recent politics in China.

Finally, in Hong Kong devolution has been attempted with some success, although it is part of the political struggle to make economic resources more open to popular demands.

Within federal systems

Federalism has long been noted as well adopted to a nation of different mores and folkways. It allocates central governments those powers critical for national survival (war, economy, civil rights) and to peripheral governments of other powers fitted to differing local values and resources. Federalism is thus an effort to reconcile conflicting impulses in society which generate a constant tension among levels of government which varies from group competition over limited resources. That tension provides a dynamic quality to such systems, in which both political cooperation and conflict must be pursued.

What is striking about the federal nations portrayed here is the effort of higher governments to assume educational power from lower governments. Most often this assumption ran toward the center government, as in Australia, Canada, Nigeria, and PNG, but it also ran toward the peripheral government, as in the US. In the case of Canada, both national and provincial school systems assumed more authority over the local system. Behind this current of centralization was the formula noted above: recession leads to budget constraints, which leads to evaluating all programs' contribution to society, which leads to higher government providing more funding for schooling — along with more controls over it. The reason for assumption of authority by higher governments may be: financial weakness of the local units (for example, Canada or American local authorities in poorer regions), local challenges to national authority (Nigeria's 1983 military coup and the possible dissolution of state powers in PNG).

Policy, Governance and Destabilization

What is impressive in this section's review of the impact of an international recession upon education governance and policy is how such events can stimulate pre-existing tensions within nations. The first result is an upsetting of conventional wisdom and of power relationships, a destabilization syndrome which appears across differences in economies, power structures, and histories. The extraordinary salience of education to everyone's lives, from the poorest refugee straggling into Hong Kong to the wealthiest American, all seek more education. Governments also know that developing this public policy is vital to national strength abroad and to economic development at home. In short, no one can be indifferent about the demand and supply of this service to the society.

Then, threats to providing their service, or plans to rearrange traditional public policies or governing schemes, trigger latent conflicts, such as those between classes (discussed later). As the Australian and UK scholars frame their analyses, this conflict can be stable until new events bring up the old disagreements over public services which are then thrown into the political system for resolution. Destabilization is then followed by a more stable period. But in all the nations studied here, it is important to note that stabilization has not yet been achieved.

Effects Upon Educational Values

Behind this latent conflict over economic resources and public policies which external events can crystallize lies a conflict in basic values. These are values about the role of education in society, about whom it should serve, and about how it should be carried out. Our last section takes us to this fundamental difference over values, which appears in social conflict of any kind. Do these local currents of conflict appear within and across the world village?

The effects of this recession upon budgets set off everywhere value conflict over the purposes and content of educational programs. It is likely that on all national agendas of public policy schooling is very high in priority, but it is always capable of challenge when national resources are constricted. It is also likely that within this policy domain that there is a continuing question, briefly put by Graham Sumner a century ago — Education for What? The question continued because the answer provided at any one point in time never satisfied everyone, so crises provide an opportunity for the disgruntled to reopen the debate over the purposes of schooling. Also, old answers to this question may have not worked out as well as planned, so that subsequent evaluation contributes to further debate over schooling.

Frederick M. Wirt and Grant Harman

The international recession was one such crisis which brought to the surface once again latent discontents and generated an open fight over the goals, methods, and financing of this service. This crystal-lization effect has two forms, however, related to the degree of development of a nation's economy. But in both forms, the concern is over the linkage of schooling to the economy, as mediated and interpreted by different groups.

The Developed Economy Senario

Parallel patterns

Across the developed economies of Australia, Canada, the UK and the US a roughly similar pattern of events transpired. The recession constricted the national (or state-provincial) budget, latent criticism of schools emerged as reasons why school budgets should be cut, while the productivity of education was challenged. In all these nations, the same policy outcomes appeared, albeit at somewhat different times:

1 Slowing the rate of increase or an actual decrease in expendi-tures for public education.
2 Changing the curriculum, which had emphasized liberal education, to one which emphasized preparation for work (or vocational education).
3 Improving teacher preparation, changing pedogogical methods, and stressing teacher effort. Those were designed to improve student learning or increase 'productivity' (often accompanied by fault-finding committees at national or state-provincial levels dominated by elected officials).
4 In developing economies, vocational education was denied as preparation of an elite, technologically-trained class; but in developed economies, it meant preparation for a working-class life — and in both places that option was fiercely contested.
5 Less influence by professional educators upon any of the foregoing changes in public policy.

Key actors in this scenario, the agents of educational change, have everywhere been groups associated with traditional values in society, usually drawn from business and industry. Changes of the kind sketched above have been articles of faith for years among these groups. They have been equally opposed by educational professionals

174

whose articles of faith emphasize the different needs of students, promote cultural enrichment, and seek improvement in the changes of moving up the ladder of life opportunities. But groups have bases in different public policies which are promoted by opposing political parties. And in all these nations the traditional or conservative agents have triumphed following the international recession.

A theory of class or status political conflict

One may conceptualize this contest in larger terms, as a struggle between powerful interests for whom the distribution of educational benefits is one way to maintain their power. Accounts of events in Australia and the UK use such a framework of analysis, and many elements are visible in the US.

In Australia, the conflict was viewed as one of a number in a society that exists an uneasy tension between the values of power and social justice. Whether the economy is in boom or in bust, powerful interests will divert schooling resources to advantage their children. Hence a conservative, coalition government will better reward private schools, which their members' children more often attend and whose better schooling provides enhanced access to higher education. Or, a Labor government will seek to spread advantages more widely through stronger support of public education. A recession whose causes lie outside its borders stimulates a heightened awareness of the need to protect favored groups and their education through special public policies, noted earlier.

The UK account uses a similar framework to explain changes in the curriculum under the crush of recession. Here there was a drive for an 'investment-oriented' curriculum (i.e. vocational education) at the expense of liberal education curriculum. The new vocational education favored 16–19 year-olds, as it was the only area showing an increase in economic resources recently. This was seen as a shift not only in values but also in the relative power of traditional interests who were favored by conservative government. As in Australia, teachers were criticized for lack of productivity in the state-supported sector of education. That criticism helped justify not only changing curriculum but also cutting budgets.

The public's role in change

Some evidence of this thesis about conflict between status groups can be seen in the US, but the use of poll data there suggests that the public in general played a large role in stimulating current reform. Education has rotated among three values — equality, liberty and efficiency — shifting its primary emphasis among them over time. For example, there was a shift to stressing equality after 1950, but in the 1980s with the conservative Reagan administration there came a stress on efficiency. Proponents of the latter claimed that education had sacrificed academic standards in pursing equality; those emphasizing efficiency could also join in this criticism. The national instrument of the critics was the 'bloc grant', which state and local units could use as they saw fit to meet more efficiently their disparate goals. In Canada, where there had been no fault-finding national committees (although several provinces used them), the instrument to meet traditional values had been national funding; this encouraged these provinces to change teacher salaries and other school policies.

But there was another agent of educational change in Canada and the US, the general public, whom polls had revealed to have seen a decline in academic performance. This longstanding evaluation grew in volume in the discussion over budget-tightening. This dissatisfaction crystallized in calls for reform in the 1980s; in the US this generated national committees of *elected* officials and professionals. The public's charge seemed justified by two pieces of research. First, there were reports of comparable nations getting better results from their schools, especially Japan. Second, there emerged a change in the view that schooling could not overcome socio-economic disadvantage; evidence appeared that it could, based on studies by the US, the UK and the World Bank. The recession played a large part in this reform impulse in Canada but it had a much smaller part in the US. There, the concern was over how a more effective education system could improve the productivity of the national economy; hence there was a push to spread the teaching of basic skills and of vocational education.

Were there more use of polls in the case of Australia and the UK, the public's role might be seen as a broader explanation than just vested interests. Would public opinion precede or follow demands by different party governments to change educational policies in distinctive ways? In these democratic nations, large change may not be possible without a groundswell of demand for change. Hence, pervasive dissatifaction with the products of schooling might be conceptualized as a latent precondition which crisis — especially the recession — could cause some groups to institute reforms in education. That public opinion role helps explain the shift toward efficiency in Canada and the US — as it does in the American's shift to equality a generation ago.

The Developing Economy Scenario

Across differing structures of politics and economics, China, Hong Kong, Nigeria and Papua New Guinea worked out a surprisingly similar scenario reflecting fundamental values. The basic factor in this scenario is that developing economies generate sudden, huge demands for education for two reasons. There is large consumer demand for it as a means of a better life or upward mobility. Also, leaders see the need to build a professionally and technically trained segment of the labor force to handle the emergence of new social structures.

The first stage of this demand (where these four nations are presently) sees massive primary education programs of a comprehensive type, i.e., basic skills are provided for most students. But the need for training technical specialists generates demands for more secondary and higher education. However, the latter's costs are another huge drain on national and state-provincial budgets, and so these are not advanced as enthusiastically or as with many resources as with primary education. Add to this general problem the additional one of budget constraints stemming from an international recession, and one understands why the brakes were put on educational expansion. This entire issue becomes enormously politicized in federal systems, where different parties, states, and standards of quality create much conflict over public policy. Even within the unitary China, similar differences about the nature of educational goals and methods emerge in the top-down vs. bottom-up controversy still underway.

The particulars of this general scenario are of interest. In China, there is a basic ideological division over the consumption vs. productive nature of education. There are still signs of the older emphasis on equalitarianism from the Cultural Revolution, for example, opposition to tracking and encouragement of mass enrollment. Also, those who favor promoting heavy industry prefer more resources going there than to education; under new conditions of decentralized firms, industry supporters can compete more effectively for resources by ignoring the needs of schools. The current leaders' emphasis upon seeing education as an investment in human capital has had to contend with others within education itself who differ over the means

— elite vs. mass schooling — and each side is staffed with leading intellectuals and their own publications.

Hong Kong is an exception to the developing nations thesis because its limited growth even in the face of this recession makes competition over scarce resources less likely. Education is highly valued by all sectors, however, and it does show the massive enrollment in primary education noted earlier, with fierce competition for the 2 per cent who enter the two universities. Hong Kong, too, has known a study commission, but it has been less fault-finding than positive in its recommendations to expand education to meet demands for secondary and higher education. The report's acceptance by government and public provides a stimulus for expansion, albeit slowly. While its lack of fault-finding, of cuts in spending, and of contraction in school facilities, Hong Kong reveals a pervasive acceptance of education without the controversy over teachers, curriculum, vocational education, and so on noted in developed nations. But it still has to meet the central task of developing nations — satisfying escalating demands for more schooling.

In Nigeria and PNG, their federal forms generate even greater conflict over schooling policy and finance than in unitary nations. Both have the problem of meeting massive schooling demands, and both meet this with large-scale primary education while also limiting secondary and higher education. Differing parties within each nation represent different social and economic interests, while the national governments' interests — such as Nigeria's promotion of vocational education ('preparation for working life') — are muffled by differing state receptions, with some states providing much better schooling than others. To meet these massive schooling needs, PNG set out national goals — 'Balanced Educational Growth' — that pursued three values (expansion, suitability, quality). But these values' own internal contradictions and unclear definitions produced little direction in public policy; but the mid-1980s there were signs of their failure. Whether the political systems are unitary or federal, developing economies pursue some goals nationally but their sub-units pursue other goals and if possible ignore nationals goals.

Crisis and the World Village

The similarities and variations which this chapter has inferred from the preceding national accounts remind us once again that we are both tied to and separate from one another in this world. The village metaphor of this world should not emphasize only the common currents of social life which cross borders. As those who have lived or studied villages know, there is both difference as well as sameness in such places. Differences in occupation or profession, status or class, religion or language — and many more — do not make village life a monotonous march of statues responding mechanically to the same stimuli, like those seen on church clocks in middle Europe. So, too, in the international world, nations have recognizable differences in identities based on history, resources and circumstances.

But the village is not isolated from its nation. The French and Industrial Revolutions came in every hamlet, and national wars took away their men and changed them, if they returned them at all. Within the nation, changes in power and resources generate new movements of ideas and policies which reach to every citizen. Not surprisingly, then, both nation and village are touched by similar events outside their borders.

Summary of Findings

We have sought to trace the effects of one of these events, the international recession after 1975. We used common research questions that directed scholars to trace several likely processes and targets of such effects. We expected that most of the smaller and newer nations would be hit hard by the energy crisis and by the accompanying inflation and unemployment, because they were already so vulnerable amid a world of giants. In the larger nations, we expected that the external influences might be blocked or diverted by their institutions of political and economic power. We studied more of the larger than the smaller nations, as the former have much to tell us about the strength of external influences and the reality of the metaphor of the world village.

With the exception of China, we found that these external events did affect the economies of these nations. Some, like Hong Kong, could resist it better, and some, like the US, could rebound more quickly. We also found that there were indeed effects upon educational policies, although these effects became more diffuse, while still patterned, than effects upon economic resources. Further, while there was no impact upon the structure of governance of education itself that was traceable to the recession, there were shifts of power between central and peripheral units. These were occasioned by the constricted budget and the need for national resources to keep this service afloat. Finally, effects upon dominant values about the role of education in society were observable, but they took different courses in the more vs. the less developed economies because of different tasks that education served in them.

Underlying these commonalities, variation did exist. The basic forms of government, such as unitary vs. federal systems, made a difference in what happened. Federalism made it difficult to focus national leadership to meet schooling demands, and it made less predictable and more turbulent these nations' educational politics. But even unitary systems like China and the UK did not escape center-periphery tensions. In all nations there were signs of centralizing authority over educational decision-making, but the peripheries of these nations retained enough strength to slow that current in differing degrees. Variations in recession effects existed even within nations. Some states rebounded more quickly to the recession in the US, and some states offered better education in Nigeria and PNG.

In this picture of the world village coping with crisis, we see much of the same commonality living side by side with variation that is found in the true village. Both villages must respond to service crises, but they do so in ways shaped by their histories, resources and values.

Finally, as suggested earlier, the story does not end here. Ideas about education are in continuing ferment because of its importance to citizens and nations. The conservative reaction of the 1980s in the developed economies, stressing productivity and worker preparation while repressing professional influence, is not the final scene. For when the pressure of budgetary constraints changes with the improvement of those economies, and when more resources become available to meet different demands, then new groups, ideas, and programs will emerge to take advantage of them. Behind these future changes will be new, yet old, ideas about the purposes and methods of schooling and the young, one of the universal needs of humankind. Then, we can review again how the world village reacts to a new crisis — that of new opportunities.

Notes on Contributors

Ming Chan is Senior Lecturer in the School of Education at the Chinese University of Hong Kong, Hong Kong.

E.O. Fagbamiye is Senior Lecturer in Educational Administration in the Faculty of Education at the University of Lagos, Lagos, Nigeria.

James W. Guthrie is Professor in the Graduate School of Education in the University of California at Berkeley, California, USA.

Grant Harman is Professor of Educational Administration in the Centre for Administrative and Higher Education Studies at the University of New England, New South Wales, Australia.

Meredydd G. Hughes is Professor of Education and Head of Department of Social and Administrative Studies at the University of Birmingham, England.

F.J. Hunt is Senior Lecturer in the Faculty of Education at Monash University, Victoria, Australia.

Michael Kirst is Professor in the School of Education, Stanford University, California, USA.

David W. Parry was formerly the Executive Officer to the Commission for Higher Education, Papua New Guinea.

Stanley Rosen is Associate Professor in the Department of Political Science in the University of Southern California, California, USA.

Hywel Thomas is Lecturer in Education in the Department of Social and Administrative Studies in Education at the University of Birmingham, England.

Contributors

Thomas R. Williams is Professor of Education and Dean of the Faculty of Education, Queen's University, Ontario, Canada.

Frederick M. Wirt is Professor in the Department of Political Science, University of Illinois at Champaign-Urbana, Illinois, USA.

Index

Anthony, D. (former Deputy Prime Minister, Australia), 19
Asia
 see also Hong Kong; Japan; People's Republic of China
 newly industrializing economies of, 63, 65
Australia
 and aid to Papua New Guinea, 88, 163
 Auchmuty Committee in, 20–1
 Australian Council of Trade Unions (ACTU) in, 22
 centralization in, 22, 170
 Commonwealth Tertiary Education Commission (CTEC) in, 12–13
 conservatism and education in, 23, 172, 173
 Curriculum Development Centre (CDC) in, 21
 economic situation in, 9–24, 162
 education in, 9–24, 168, 173
 examinations and schooling in, 20
 financing of education in, 14–16, 168
 Labor policy in, 14, 21–3
 Martin Committee in, 19
 media and national education policies in, 17–21
 national and state responsibilities in, 170
 participation patterns in education in, 12–13
 post-secondary education in, 11–13, 16–17, 18–19
 primary education in, 11
 private and public sector education in, 17
 and recession, 9–24, 163
 Schools Commission in, 14
 secondary education in, 11–13, 22
 statistics on education in, 11–16
 teacher preparation in, 20–1
 teachers and Labor party policies in, 22–3
 tertiary education in, *see* Australia, post-secondary education in
 transition programmes in, 16
 Williams Committee in, 19
 youth employment in, 13, 16, 18–19

Bell, T. (Secretary, US Department of Education), 136
British North American Act (1867), 43

Callaghan, J. (former Prime Minister, UK), 153
Canada
 centralization and educational policy in, 33, 36–7, 43–5, 170
 conservatism and education in, 172